I0467734

Famous Chinese Character Tattoos Drawing Guide

Learn How To Draw Chinese Character Tattoos

Character Tattoos

By : Gala Publication

2

Published By :

Gala Publication
© Copyright 2015 – Gala Publication

ISBN-13: **978-1522707547**
ISBN-10: **1522707549**

Table of Contents

4

BETTY BOOP
TATTOO

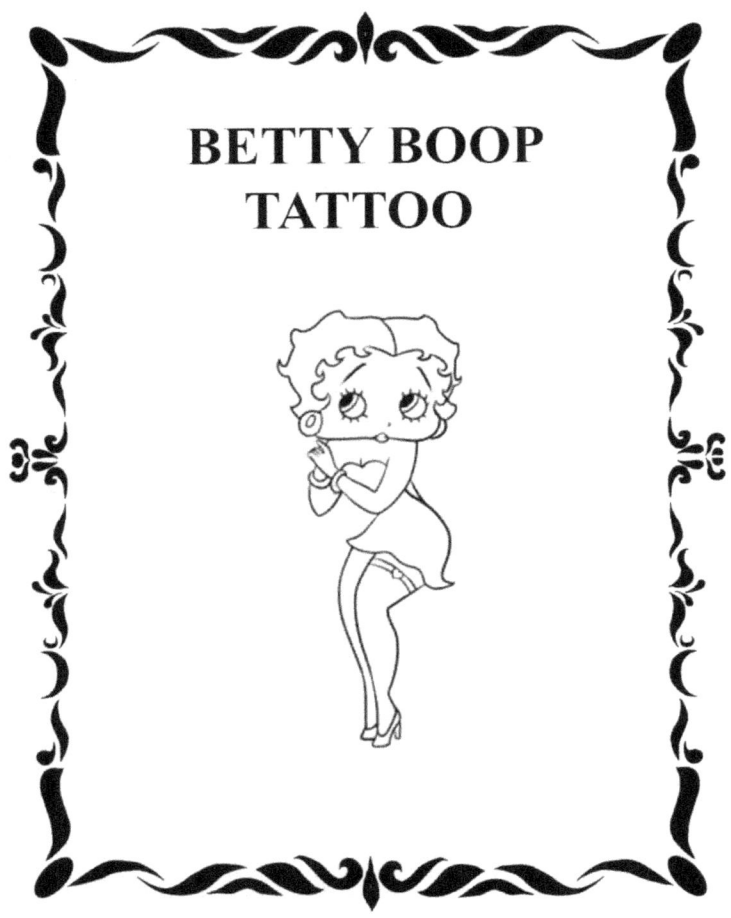

6

STEP 1

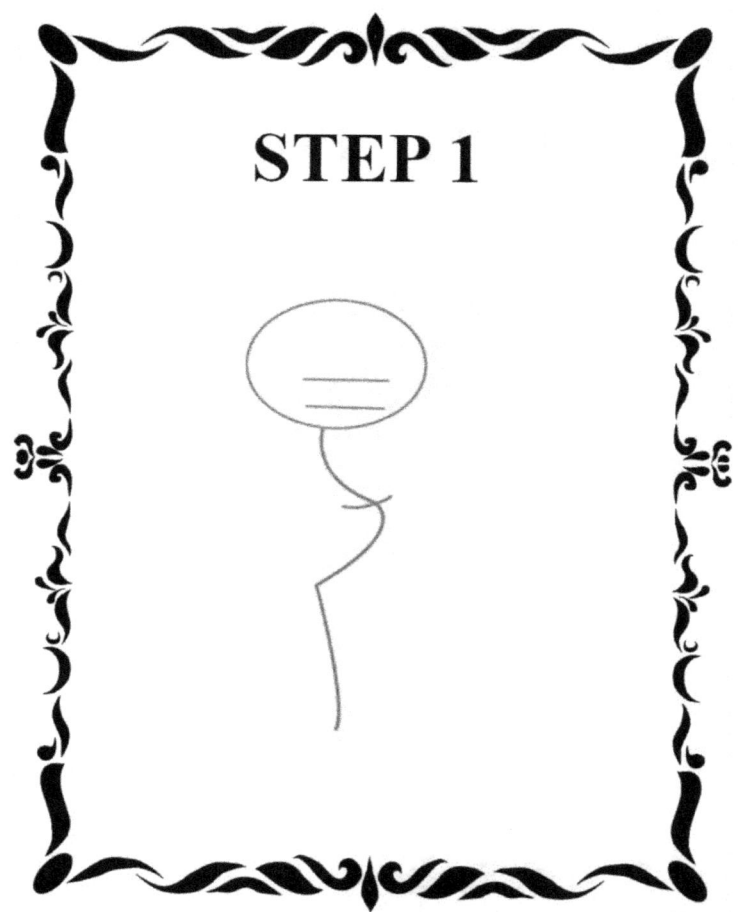

STEP 2

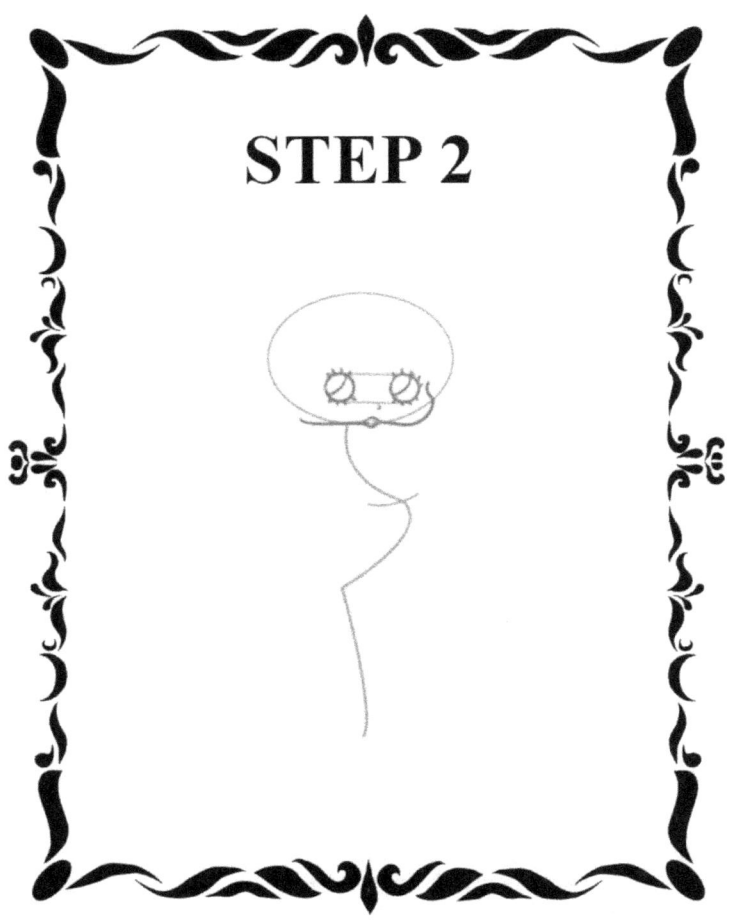

STEP 3

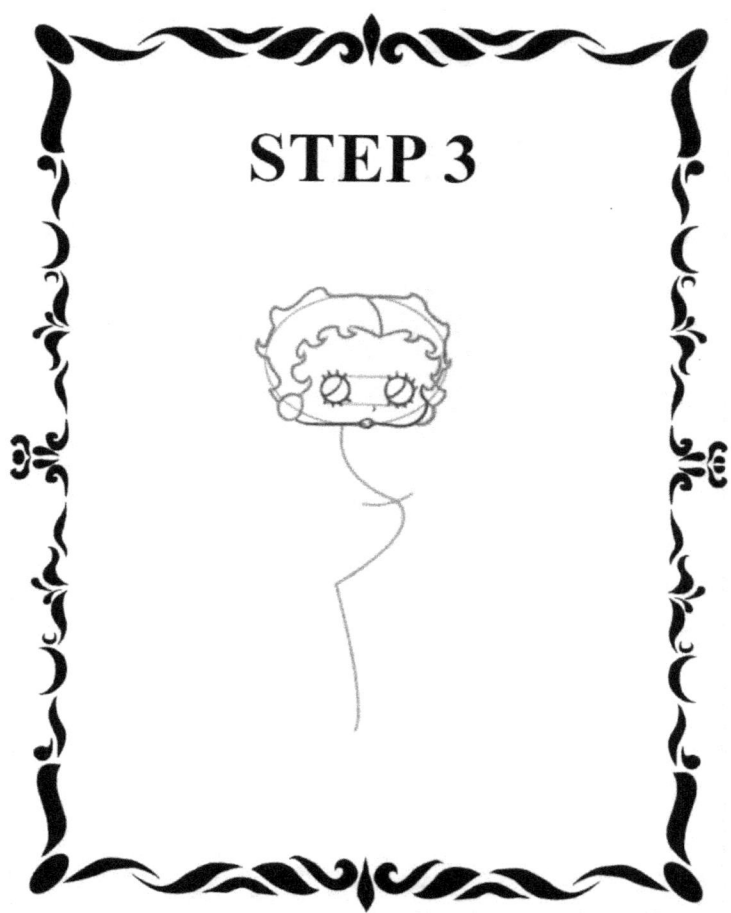

STEP 4

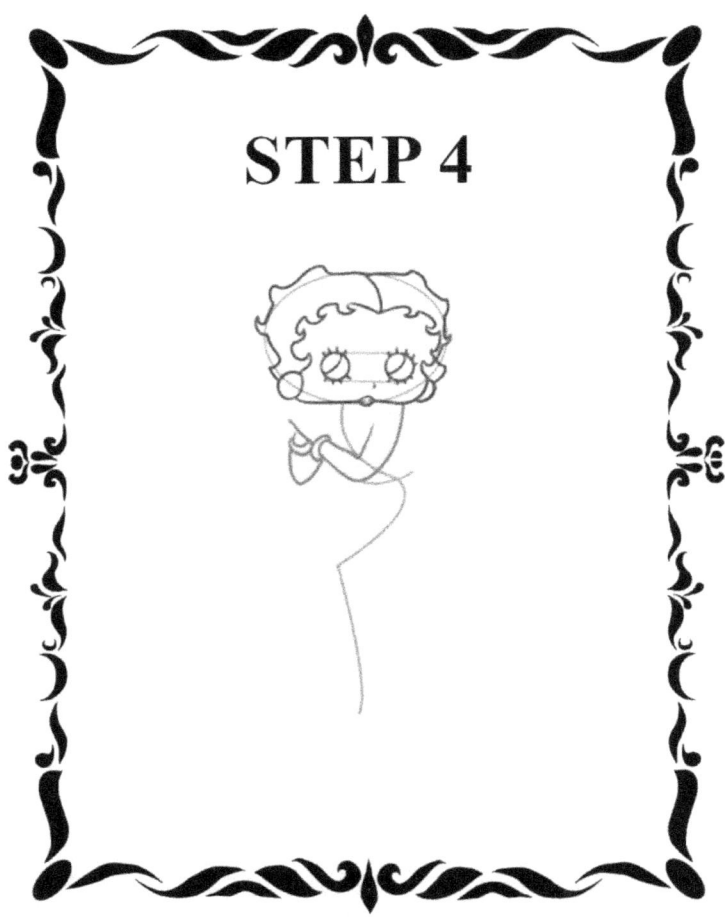

STEP 5

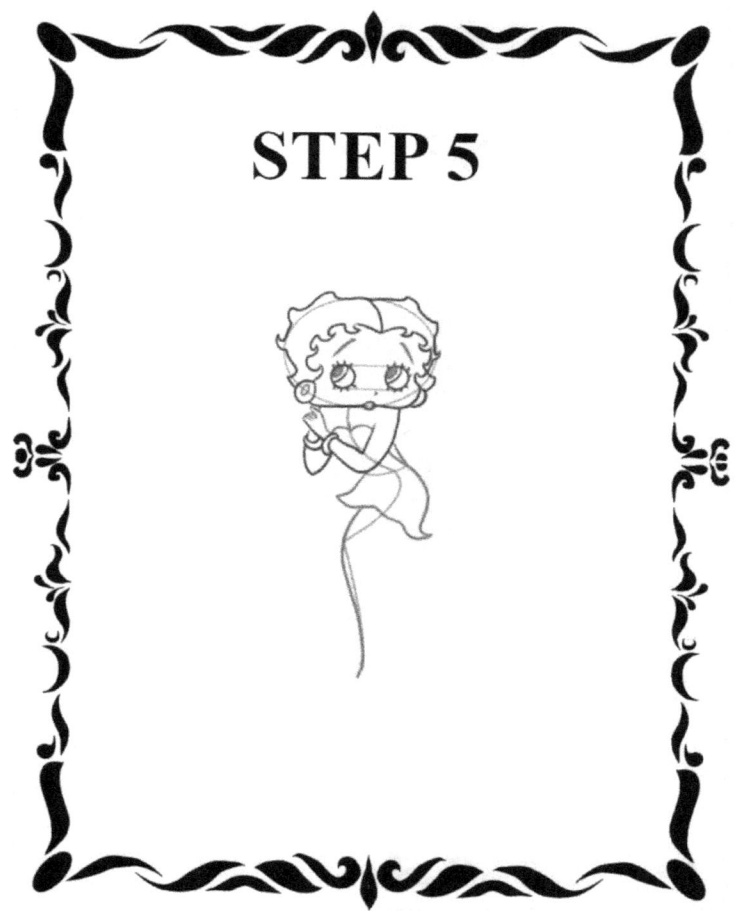

STEP 6

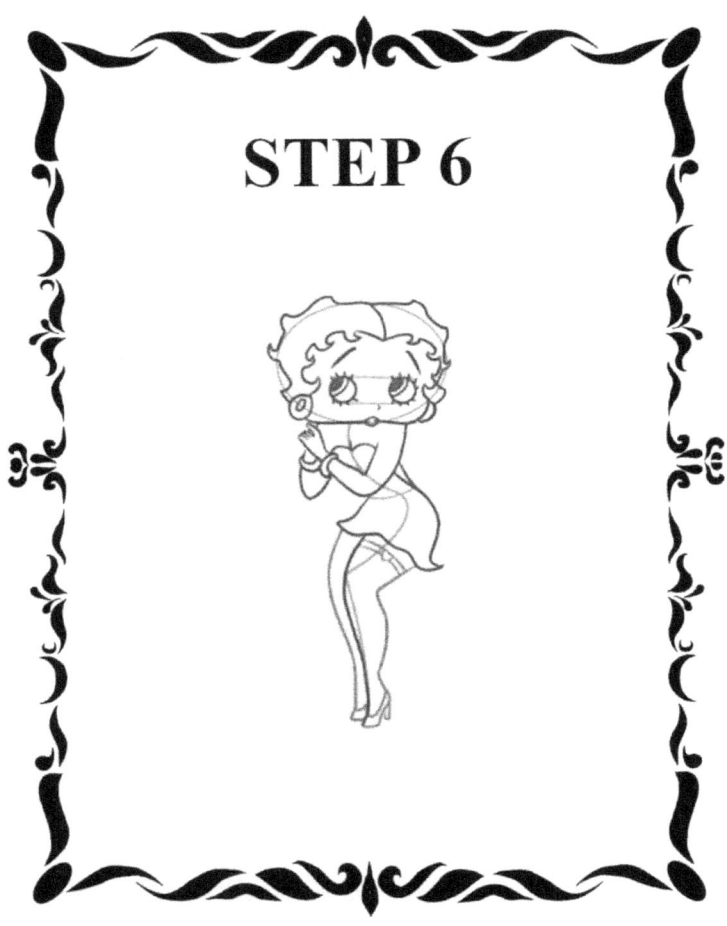

STEP 7

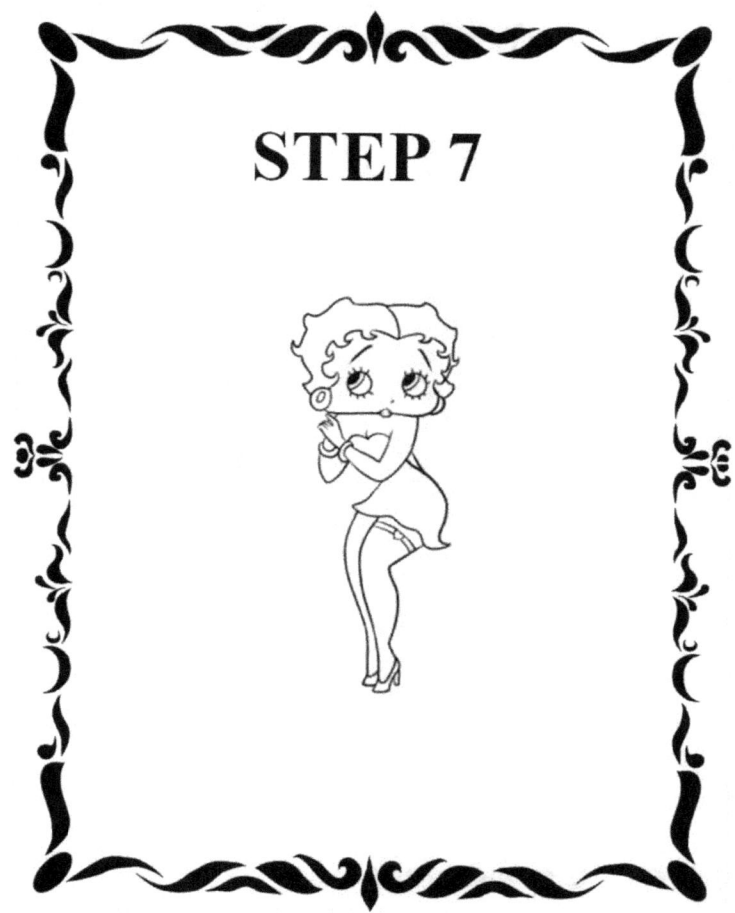

DEATH
TATTOO

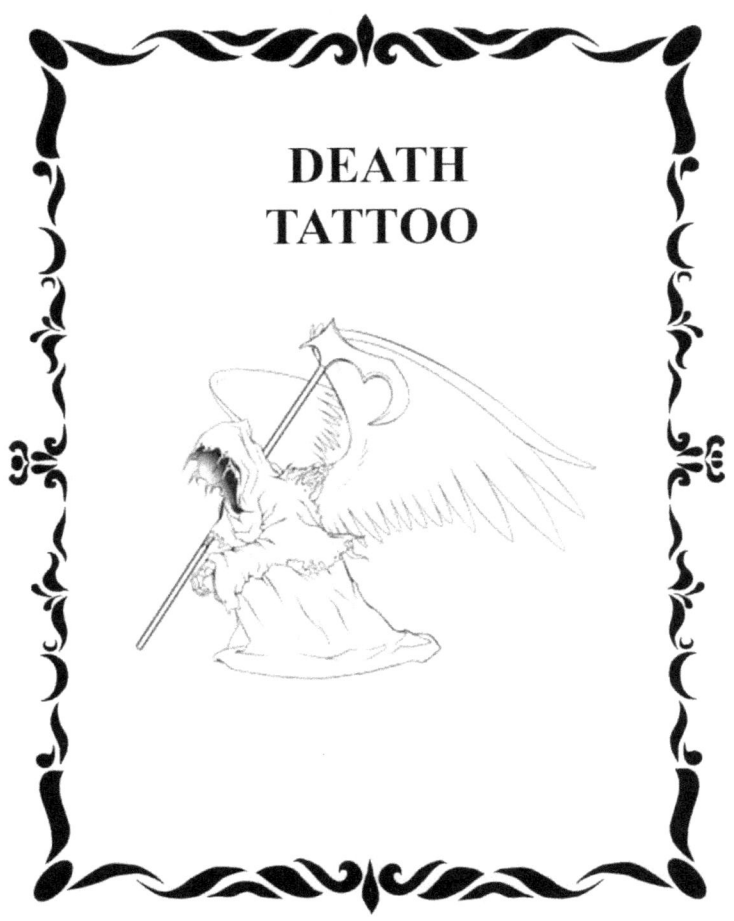

STEP 1

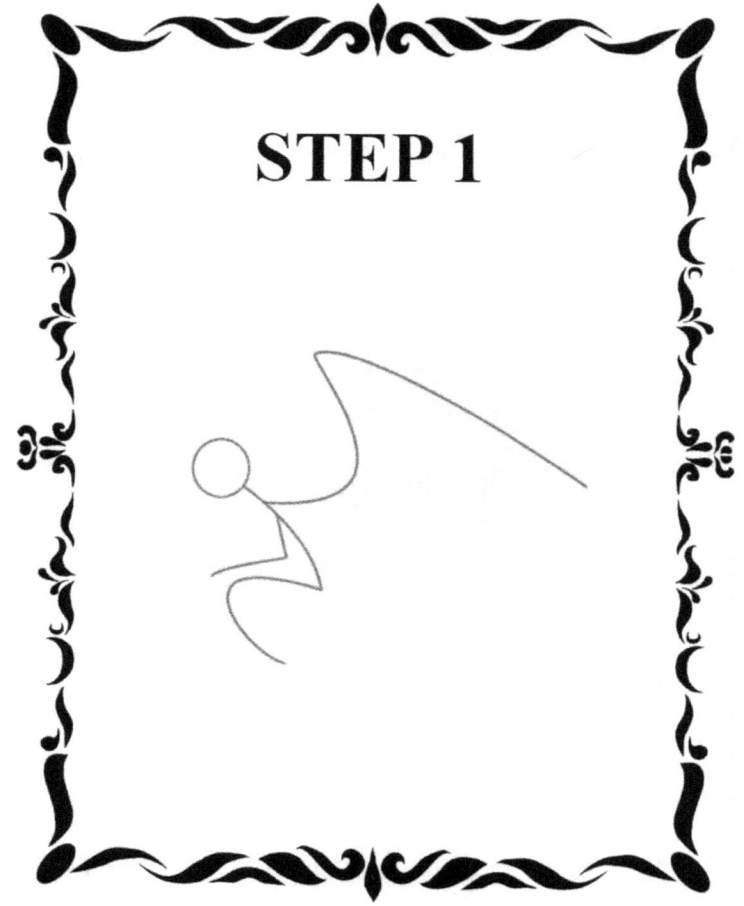

STEP 2

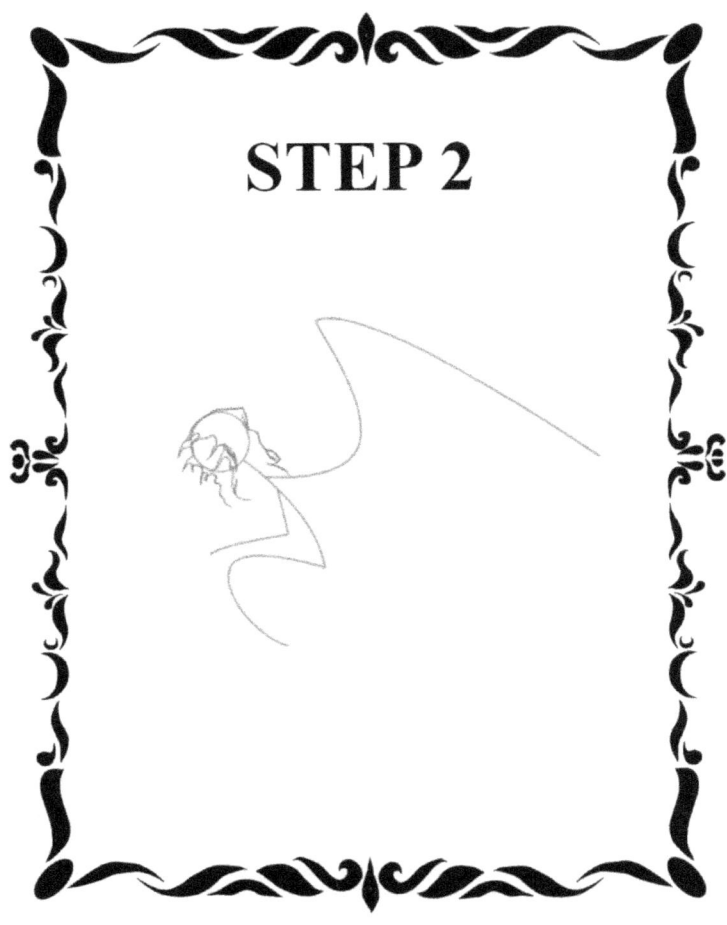

STEP 3

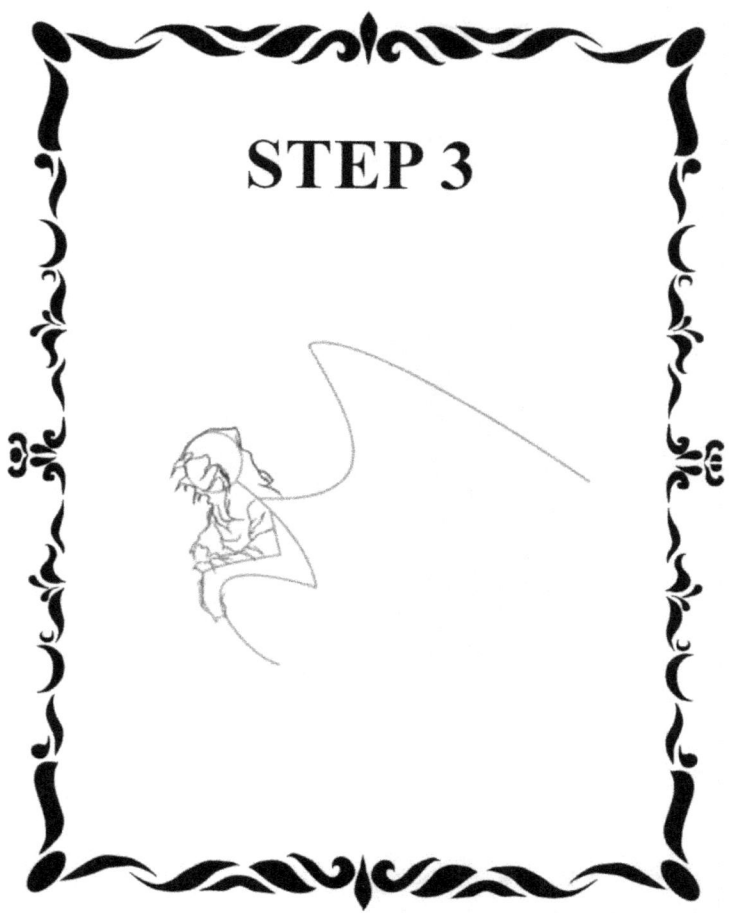

STEP 4

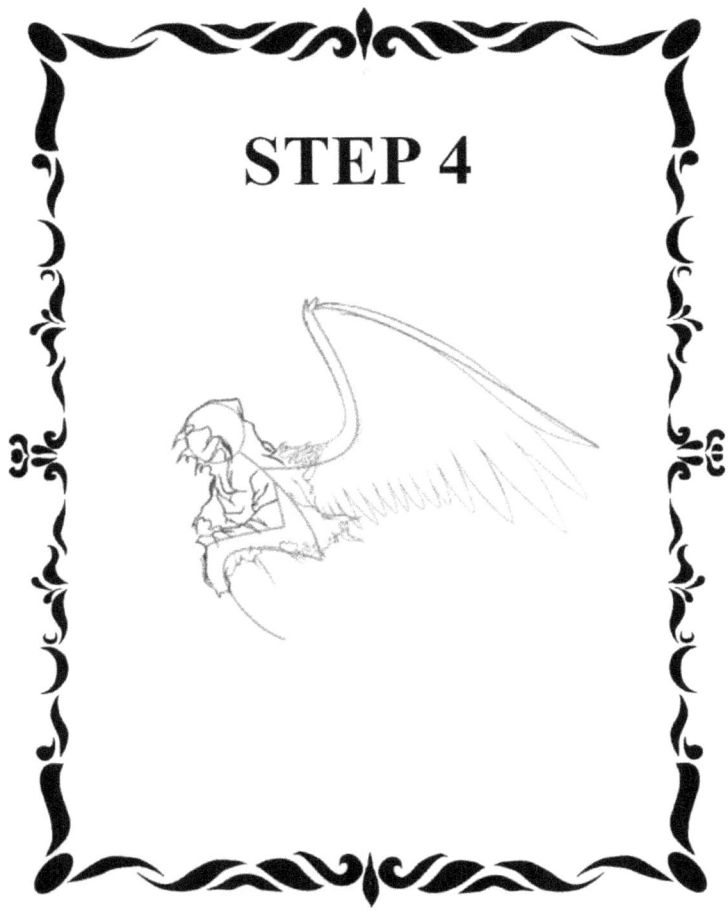

STEP 5

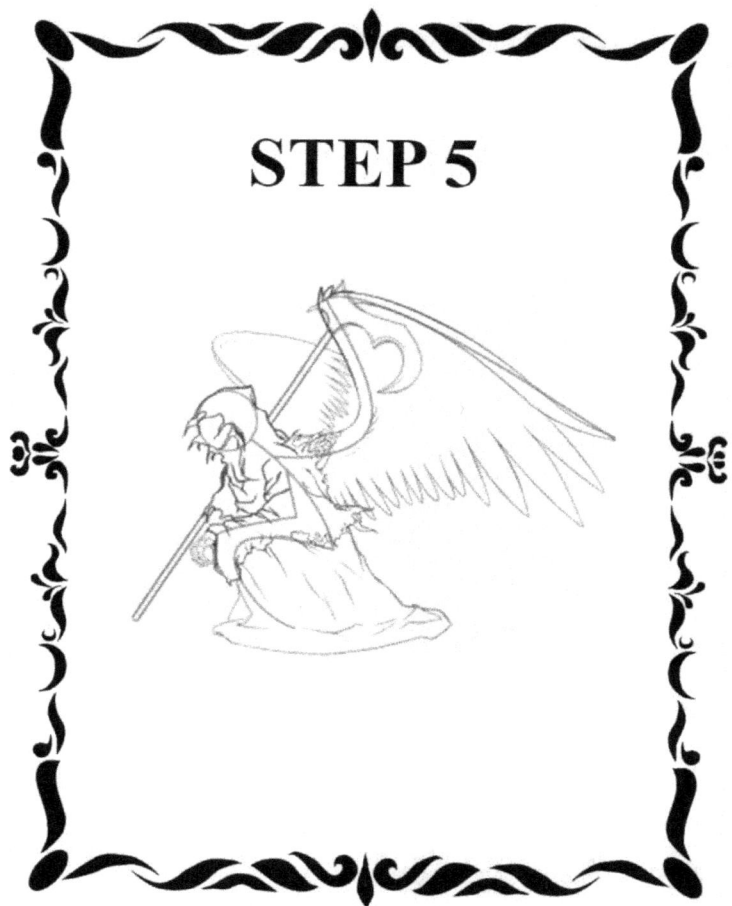

STEP 6

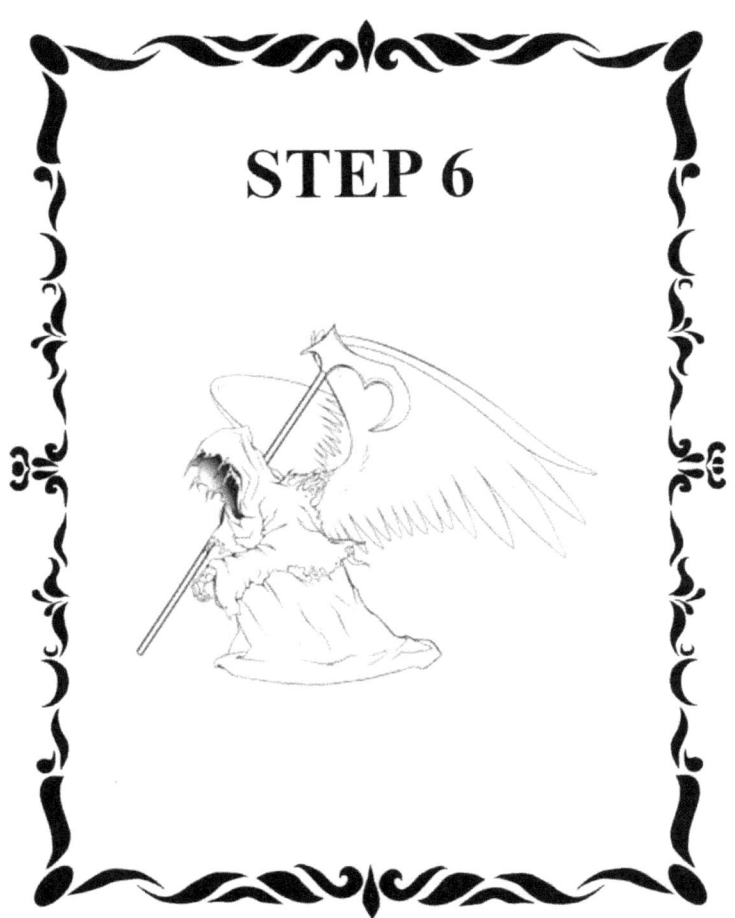

DEMON
TATTOO

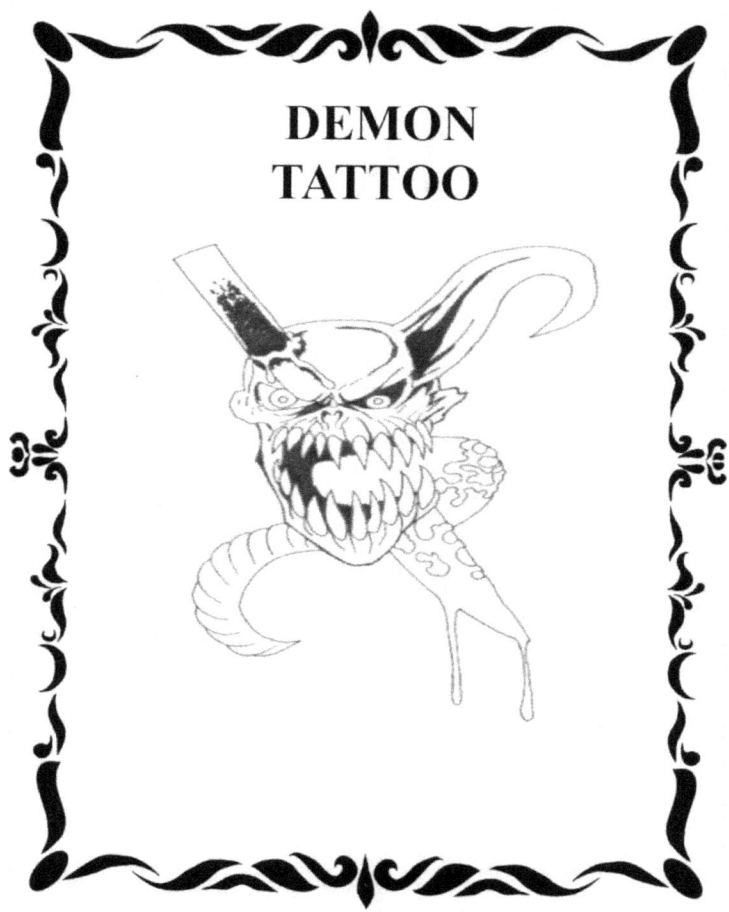

STEP 1

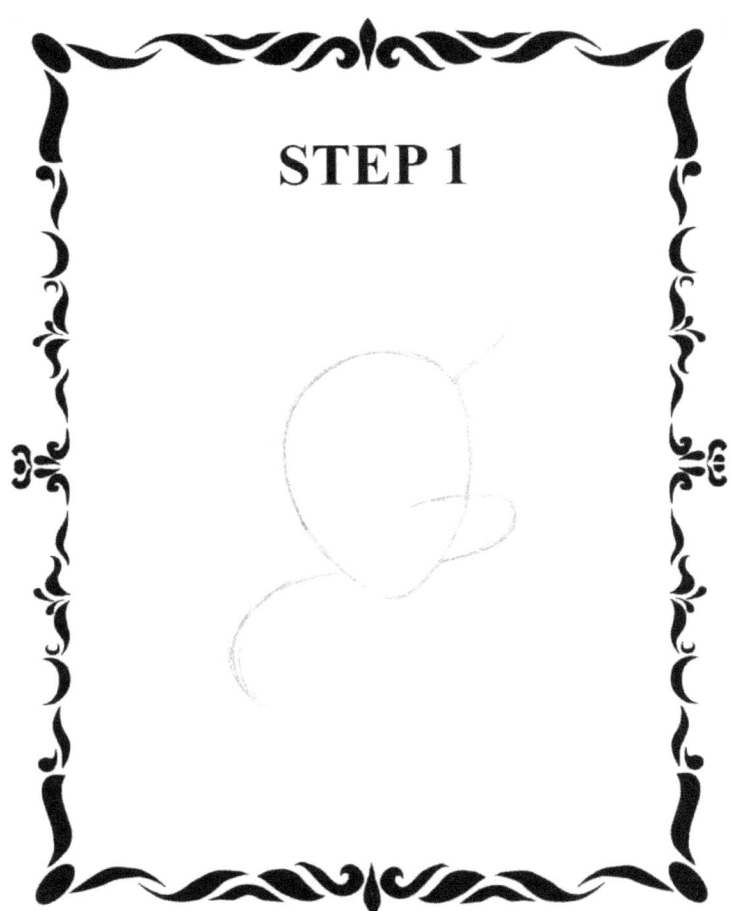

STEP 2

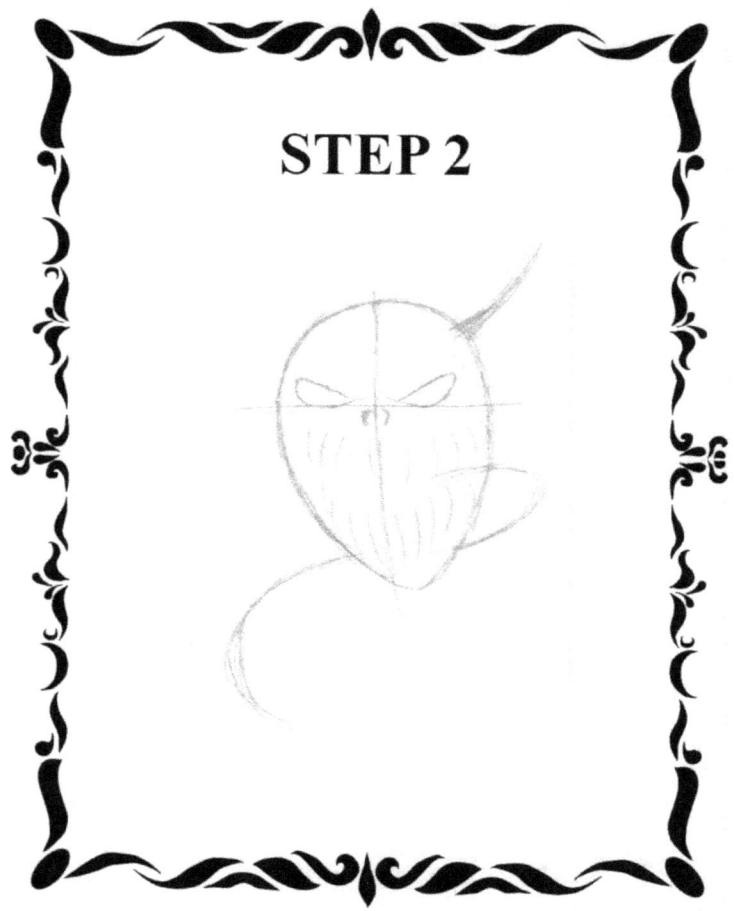

STEP 3

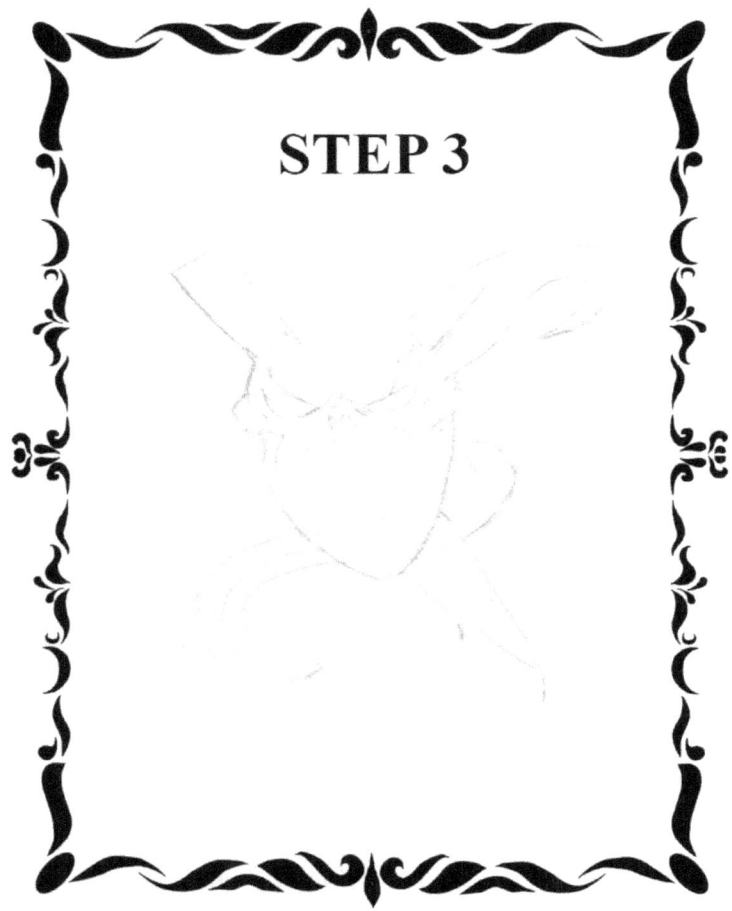

STEP 4

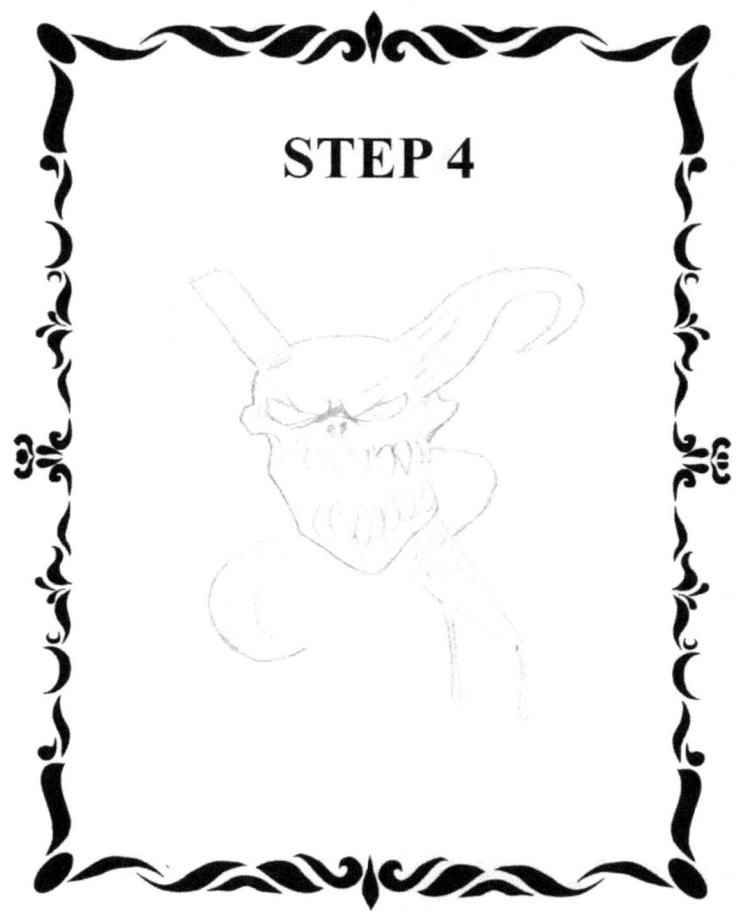

STEP 5

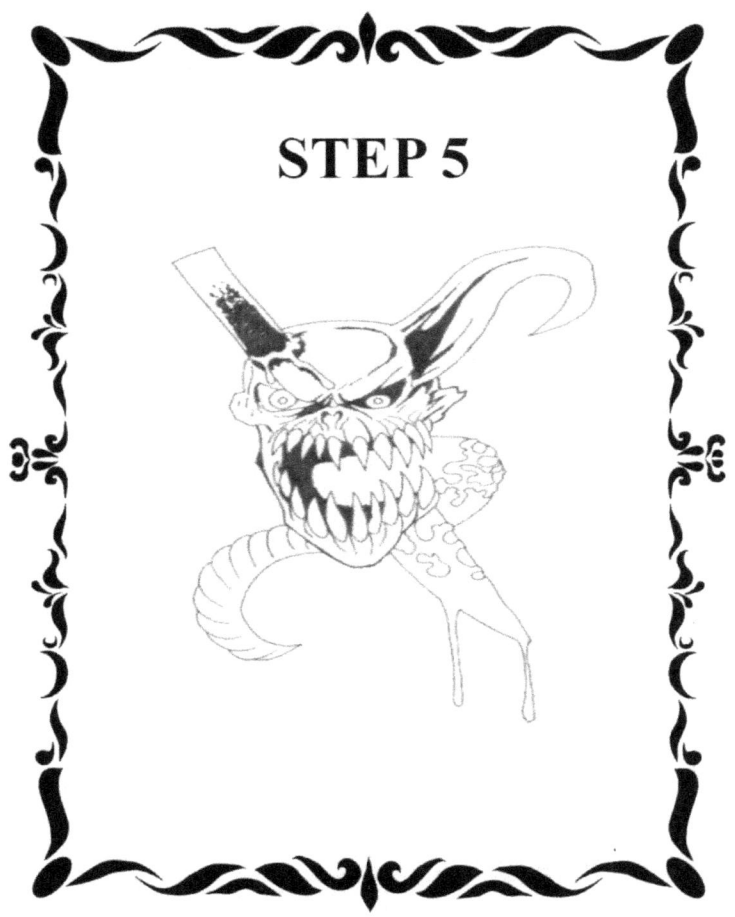

DEVIL TATTOO

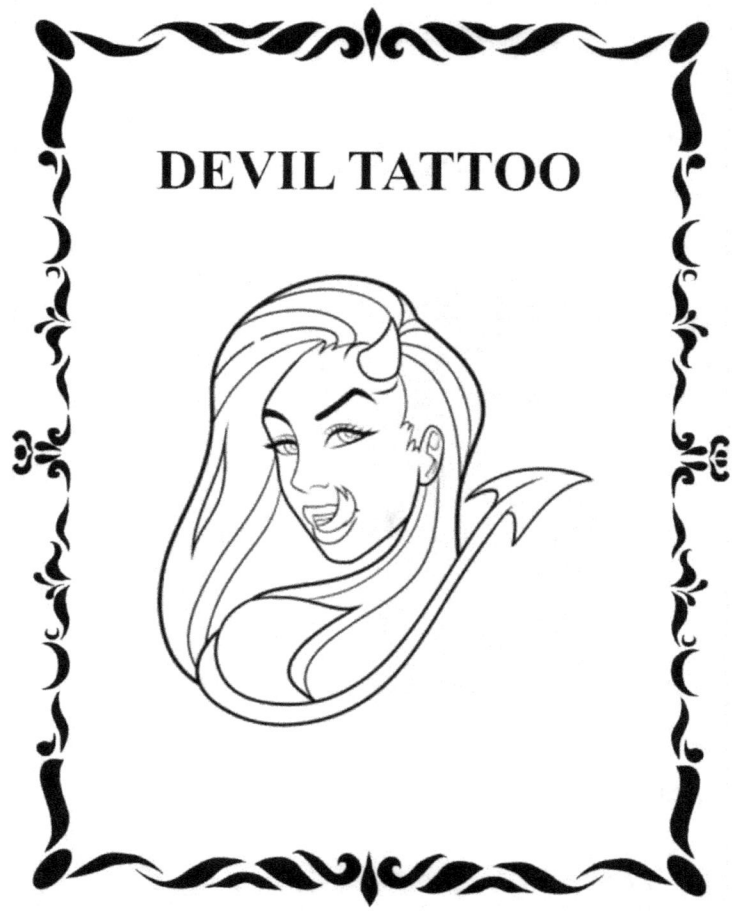

STEP 1

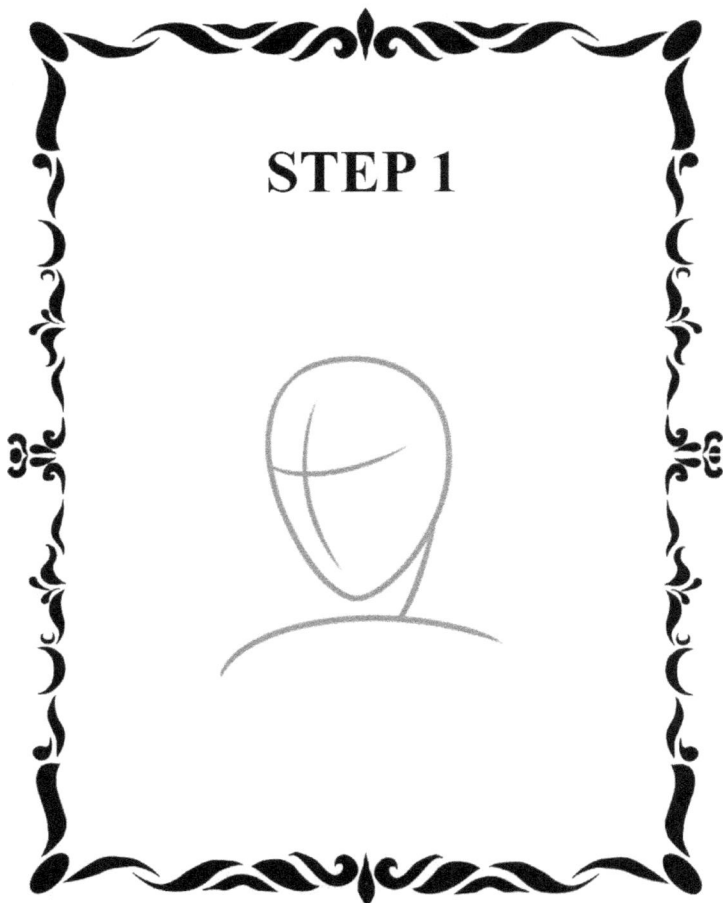

STEP 2

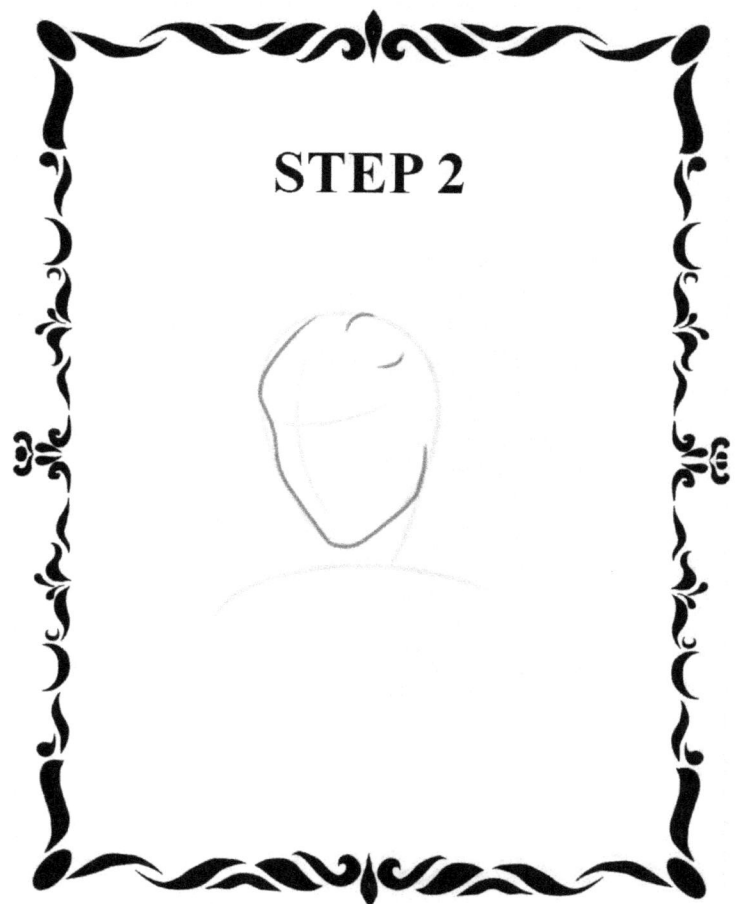

STEP 3

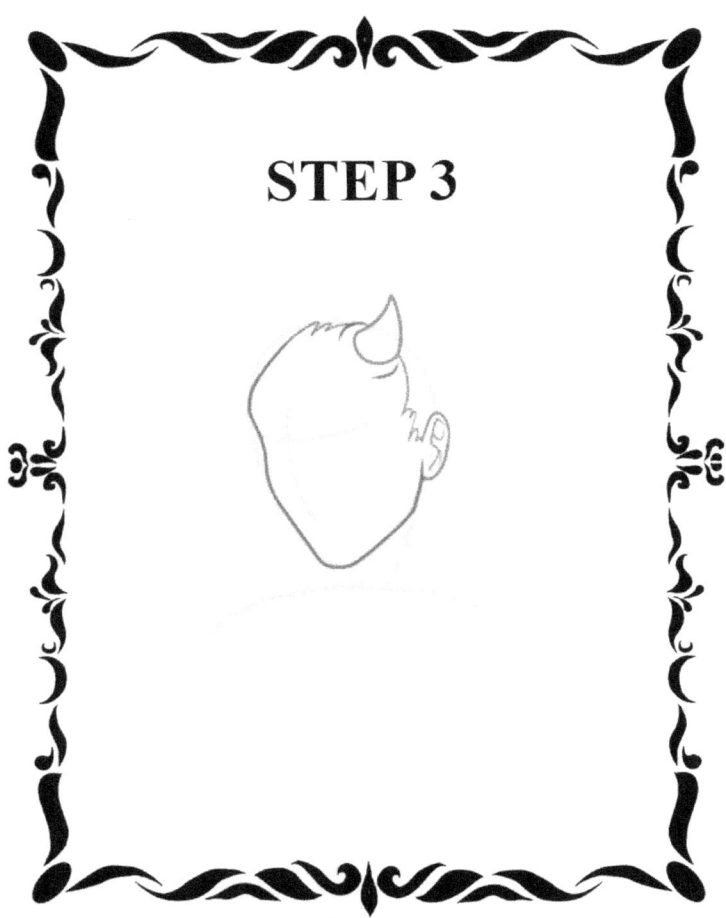

STEP 4

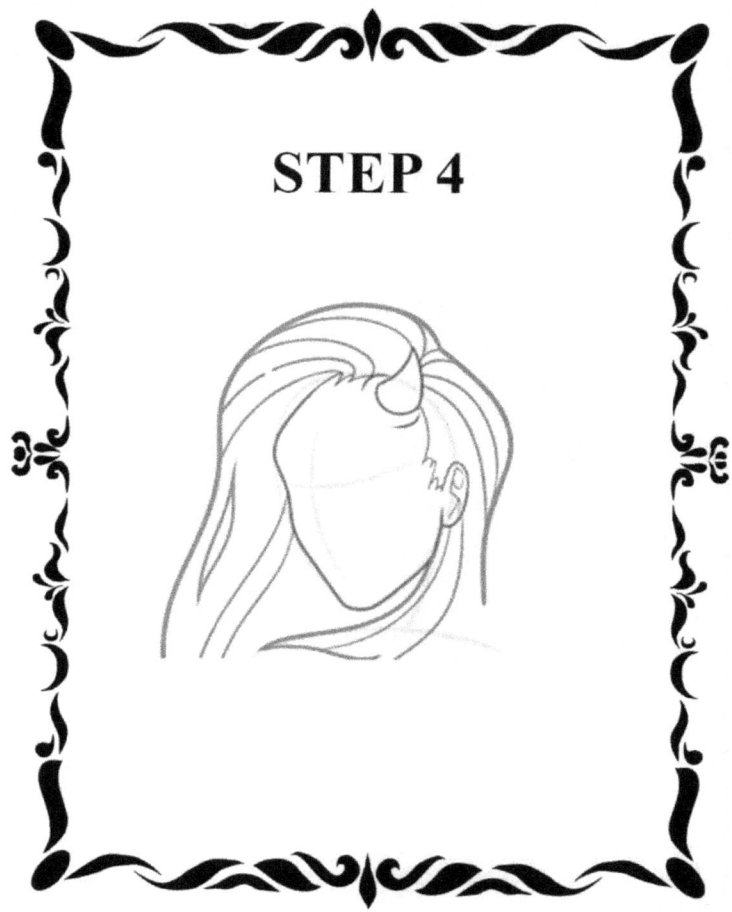

STEP 5

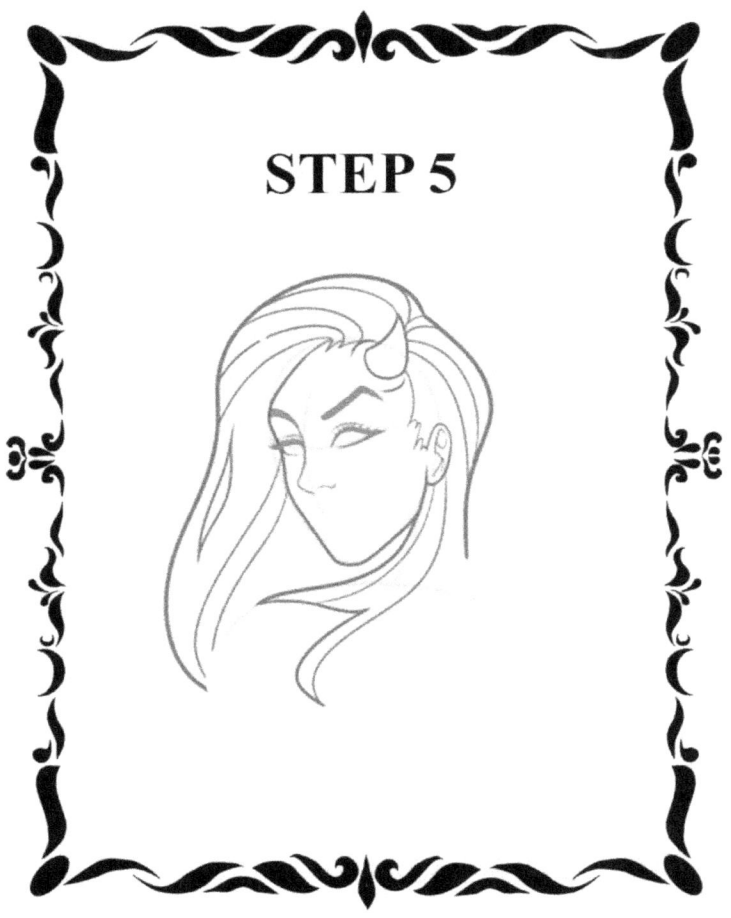

STEP 6

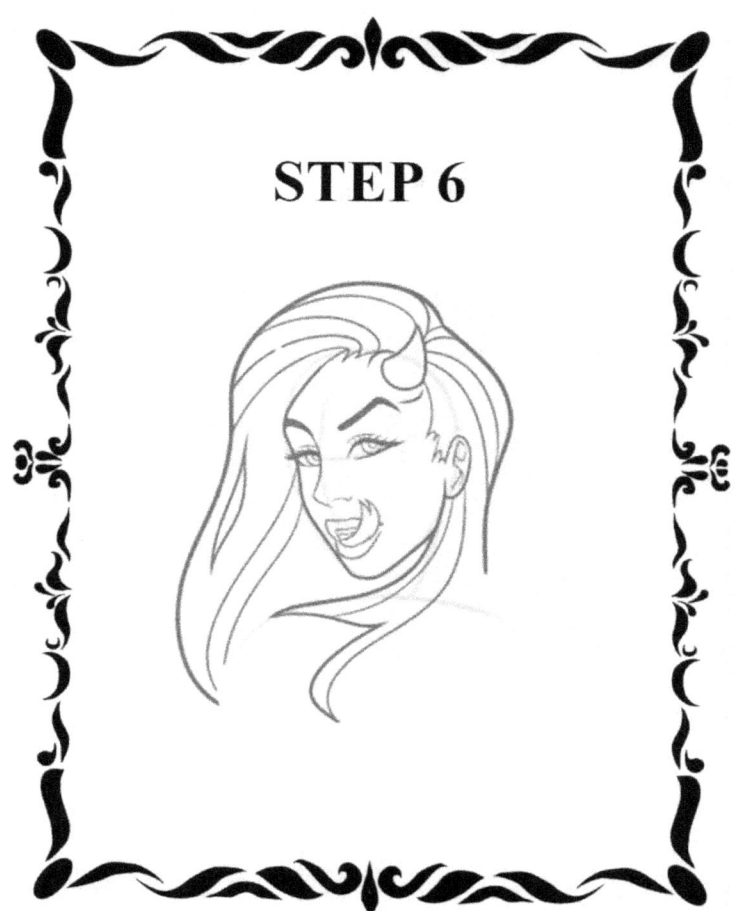

STEP 7

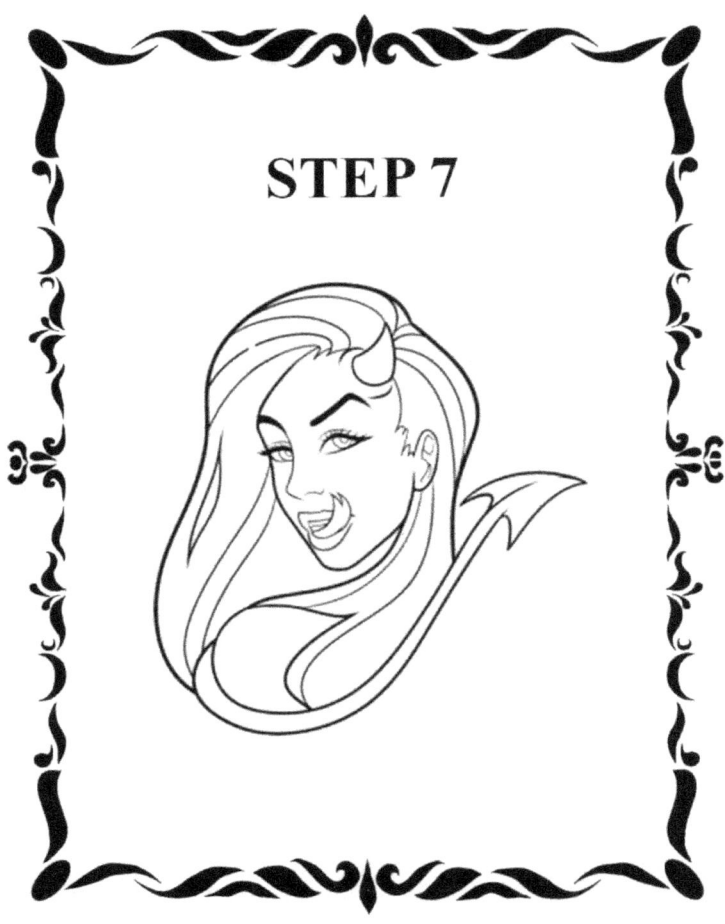

FAIRY TATTOO

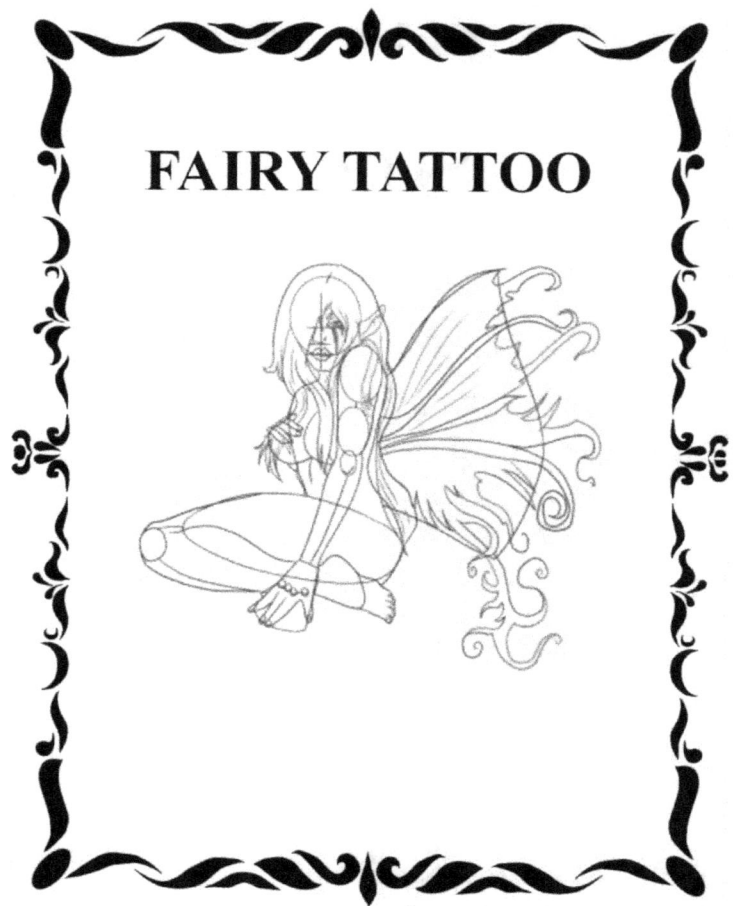

STEP 1

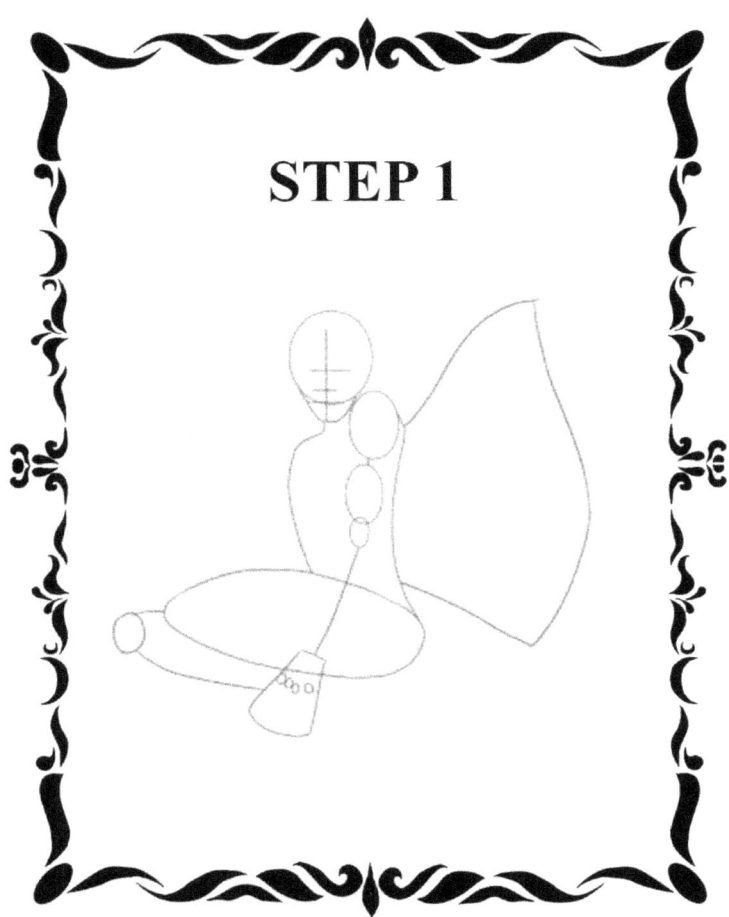

STEP 2

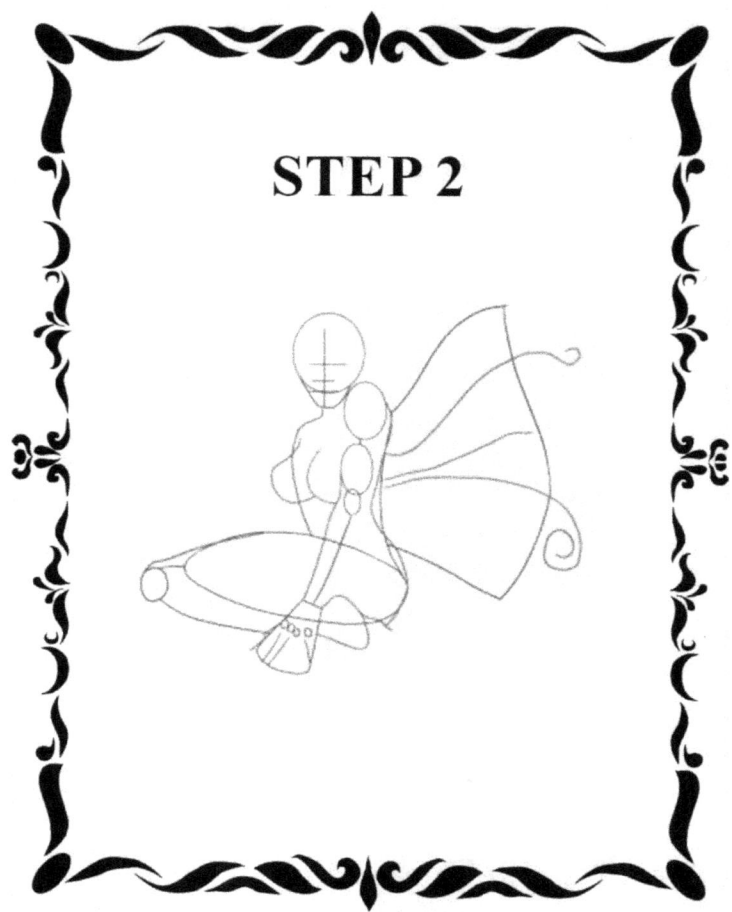

STEP 3

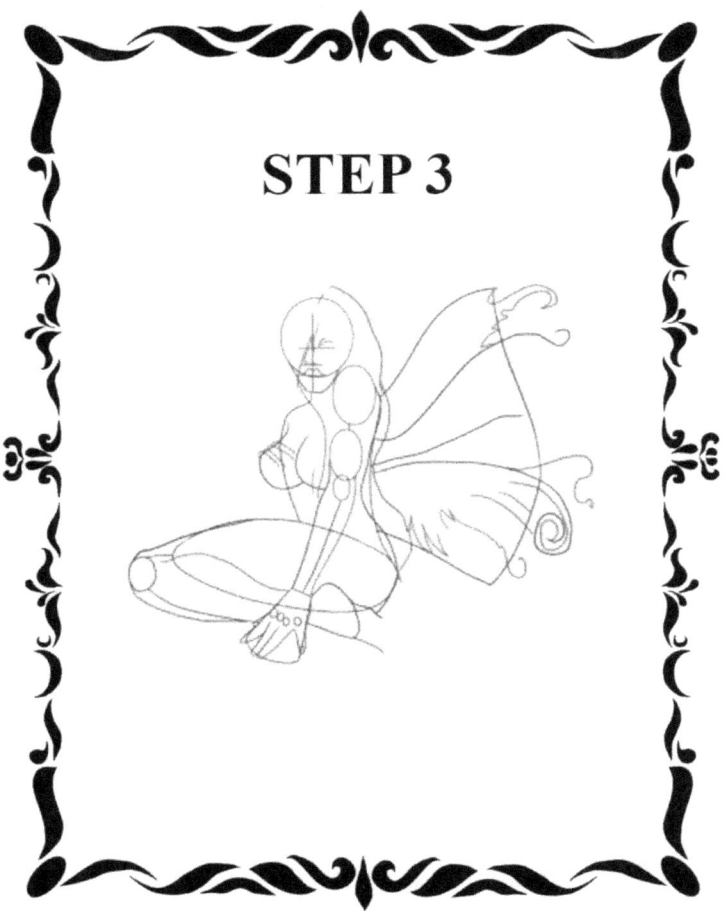

STEP 4

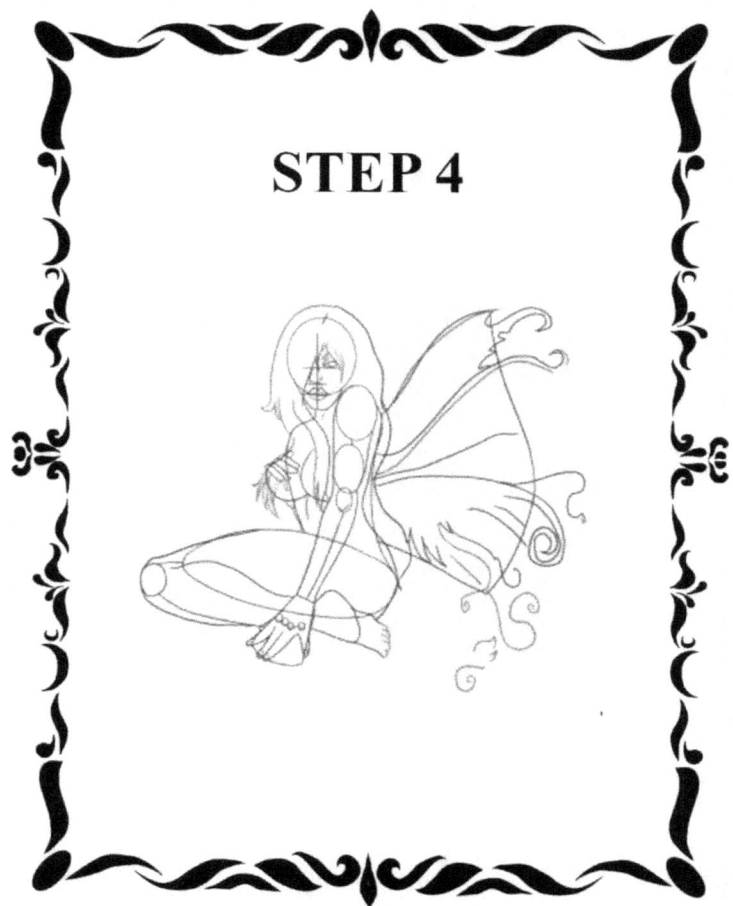

STEP 5

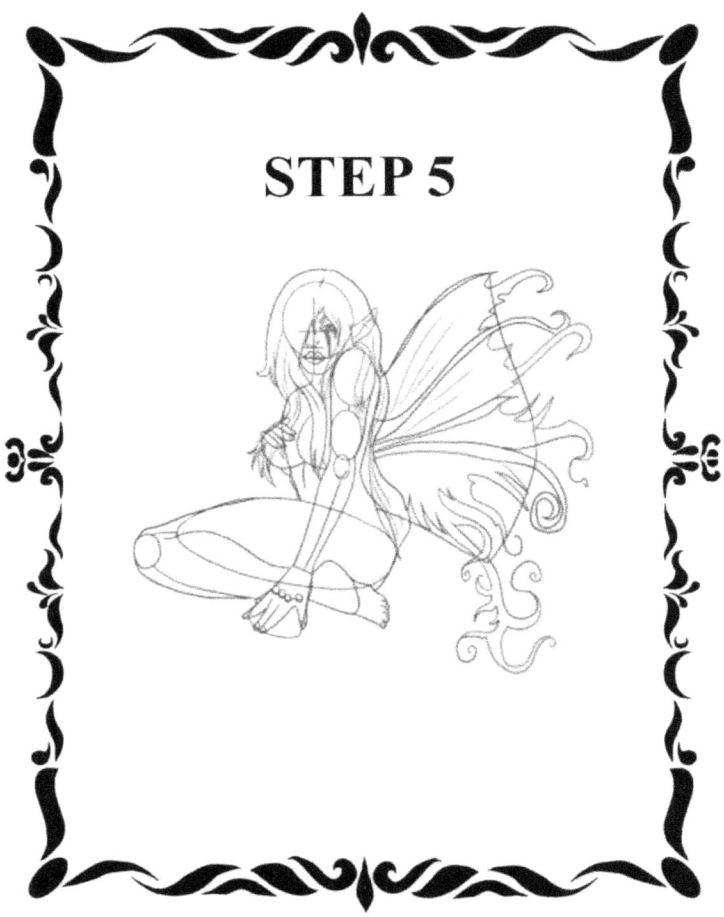

GRIM REAPER TATTOO

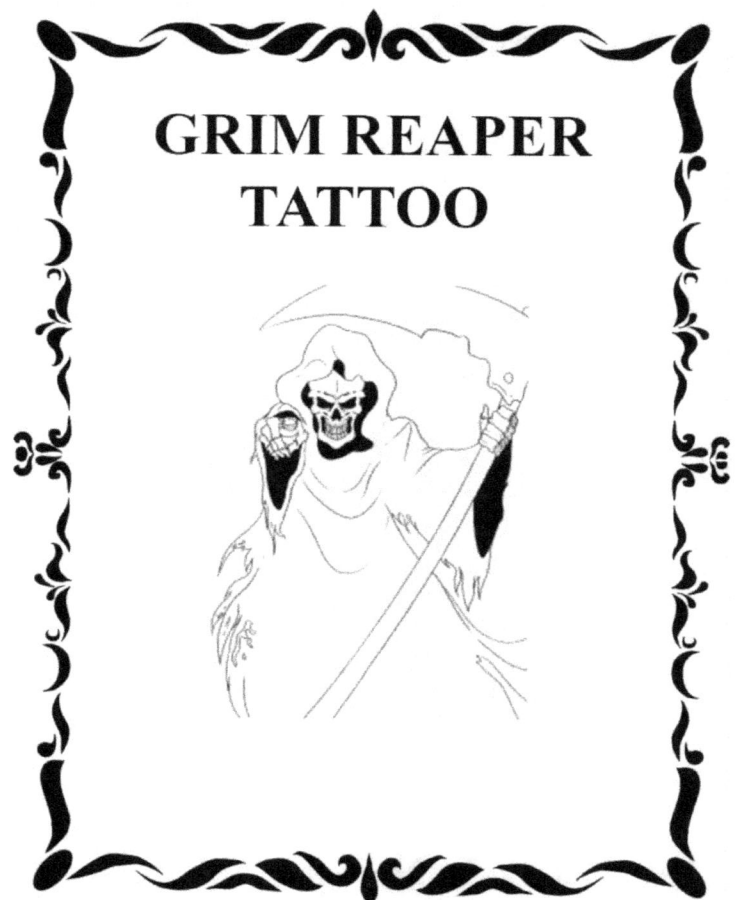

STEP 1

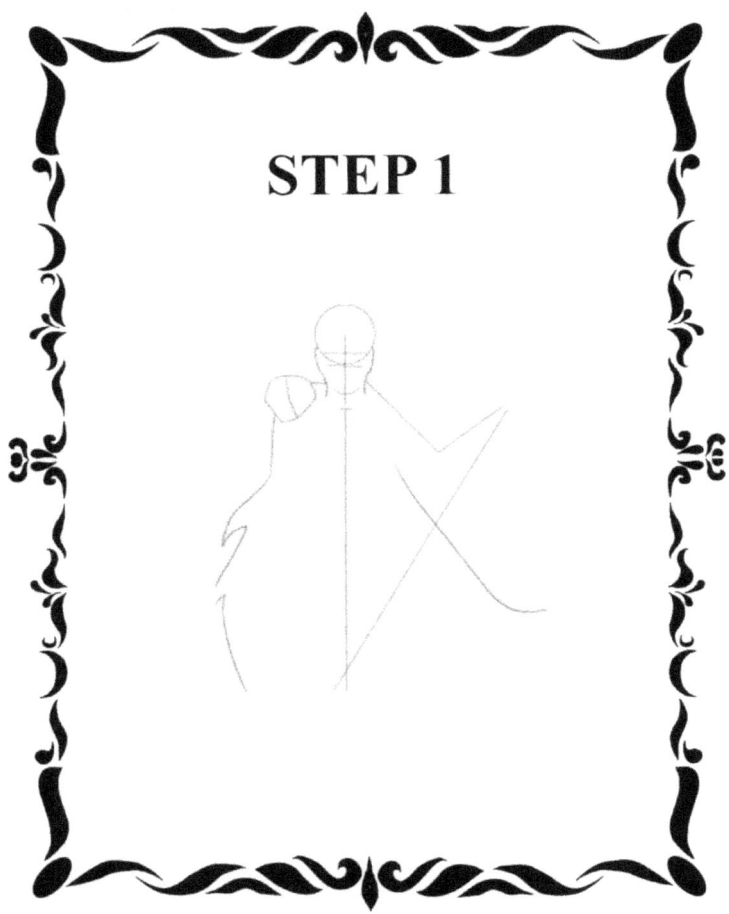

STEP 2

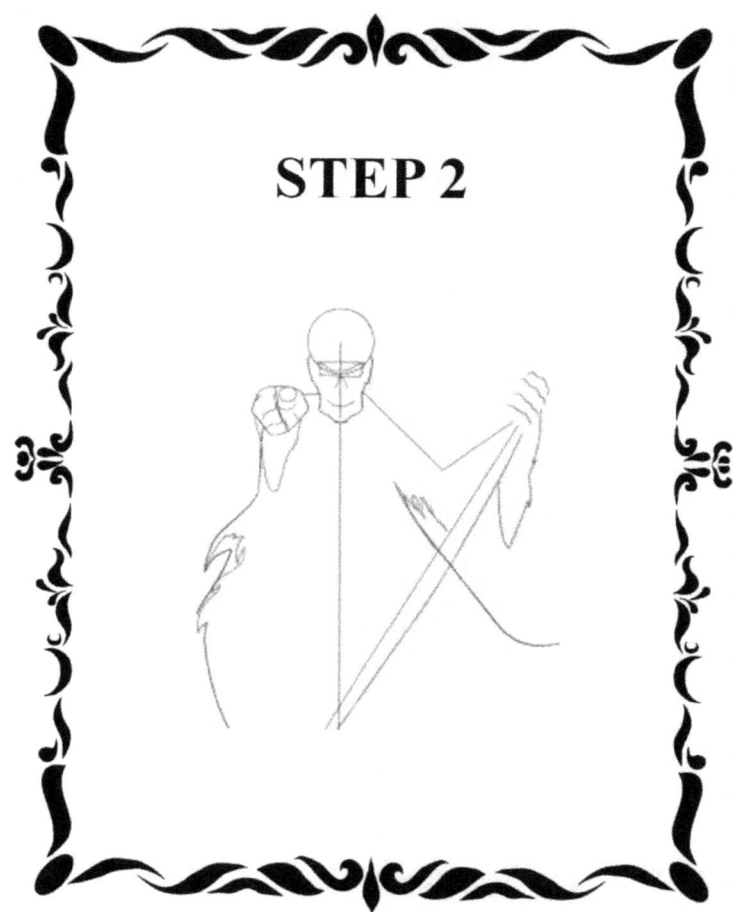

STEP 3

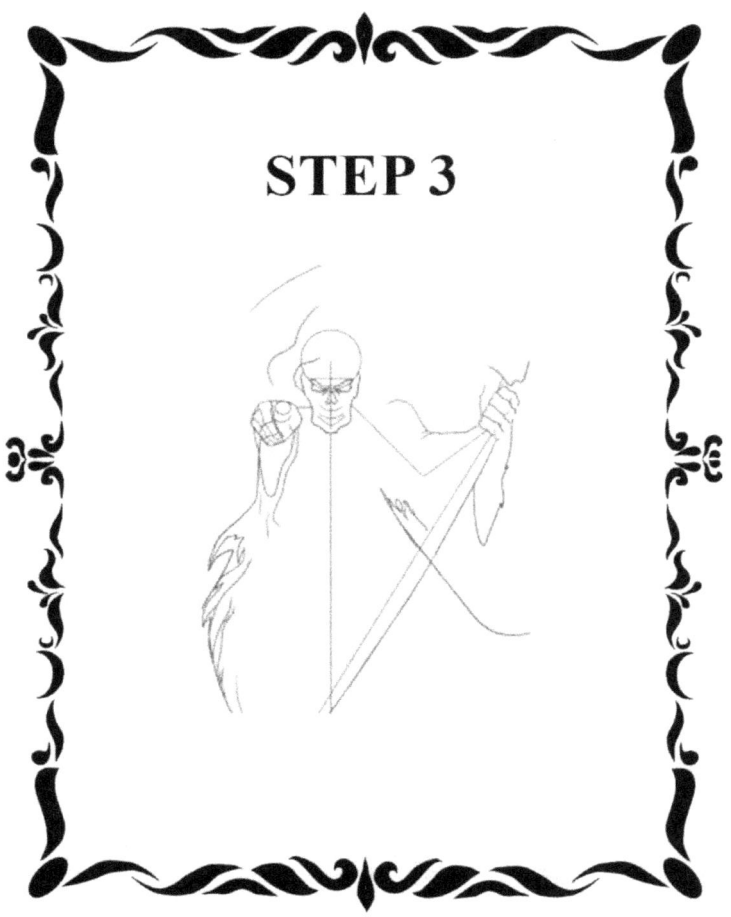

STEP 4

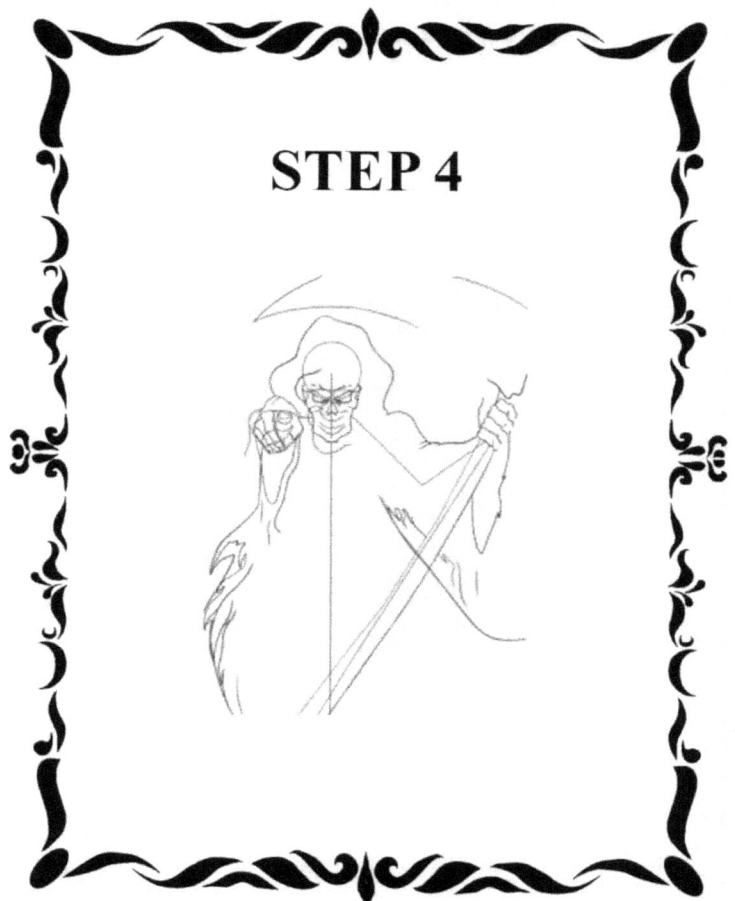

STEP 5

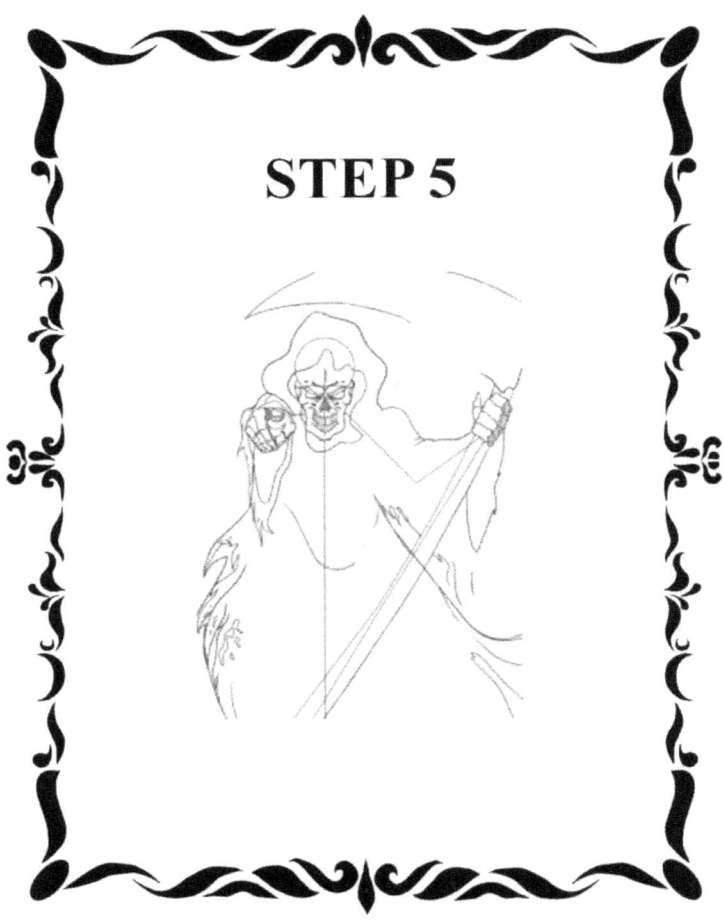

STEP 6

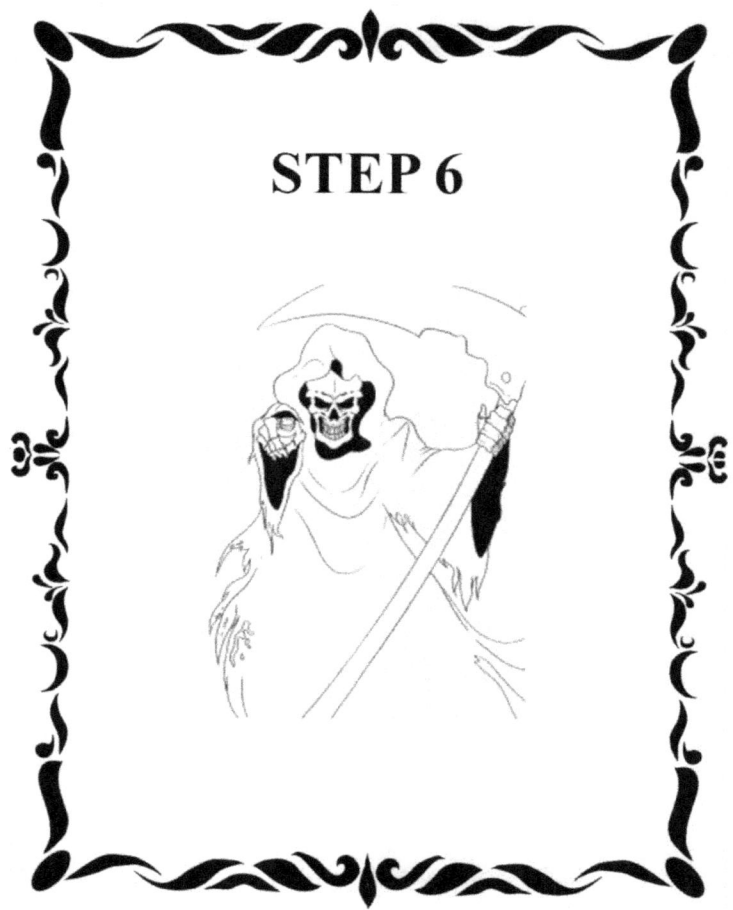

JOKER TATTOO

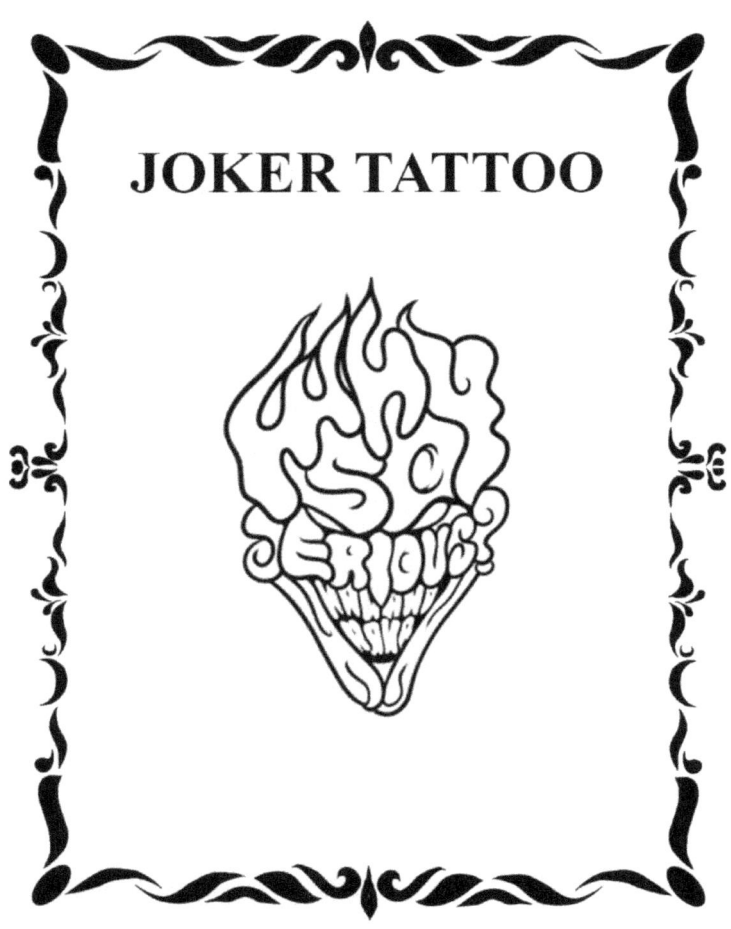

STEP 1

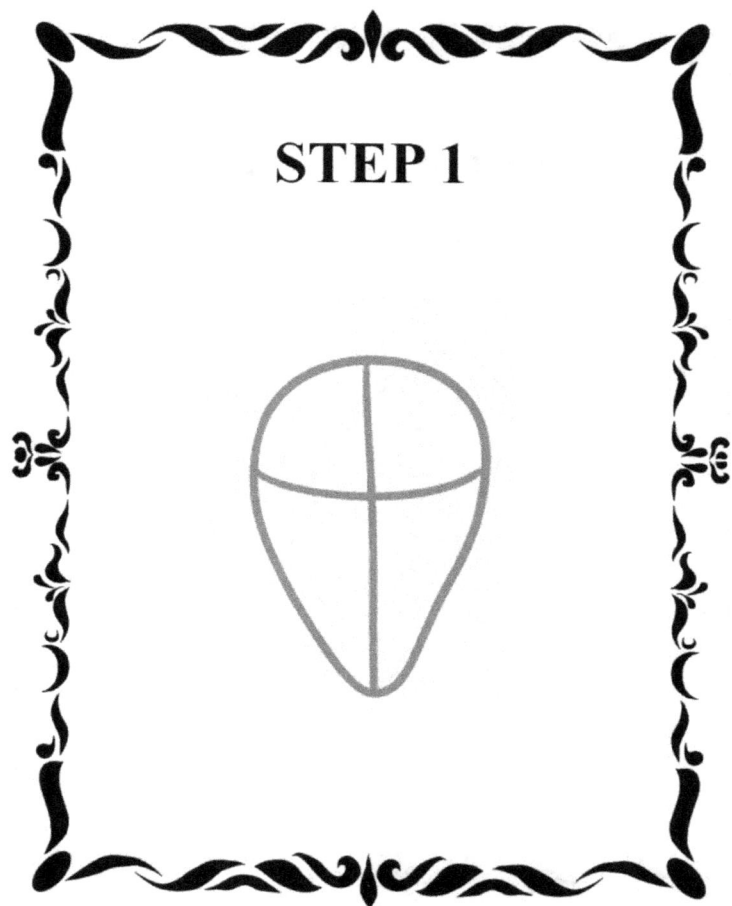

STEP 2

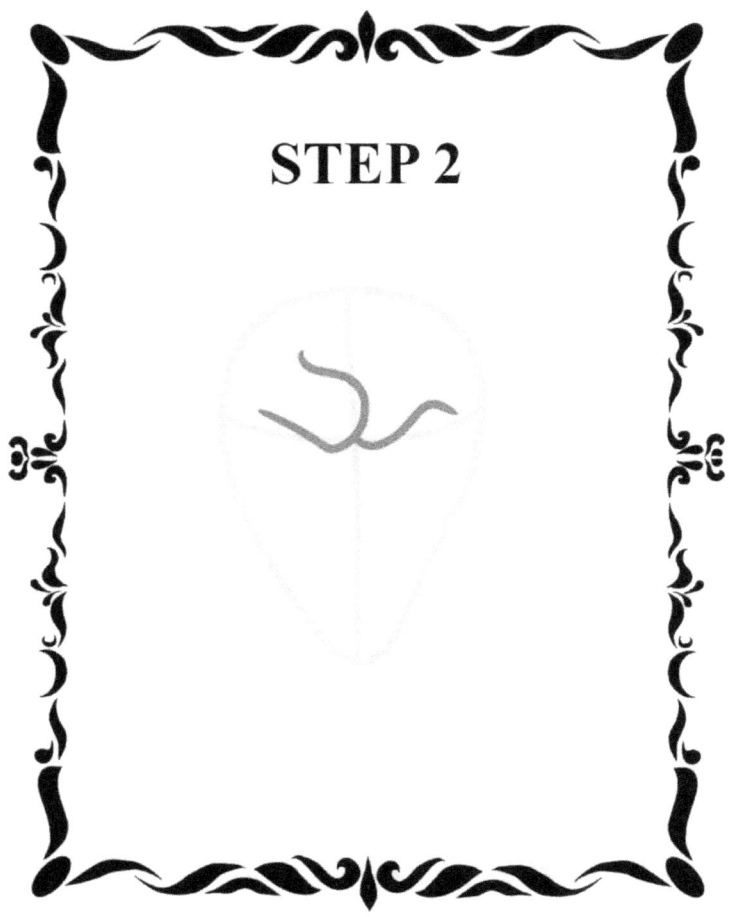

STEP 3

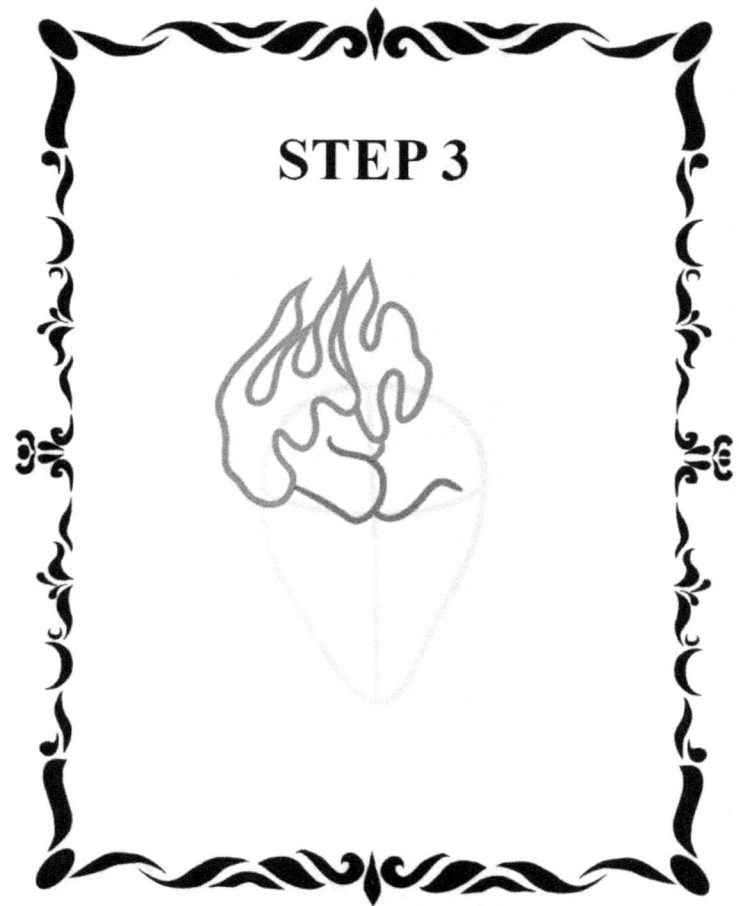

STEP 4

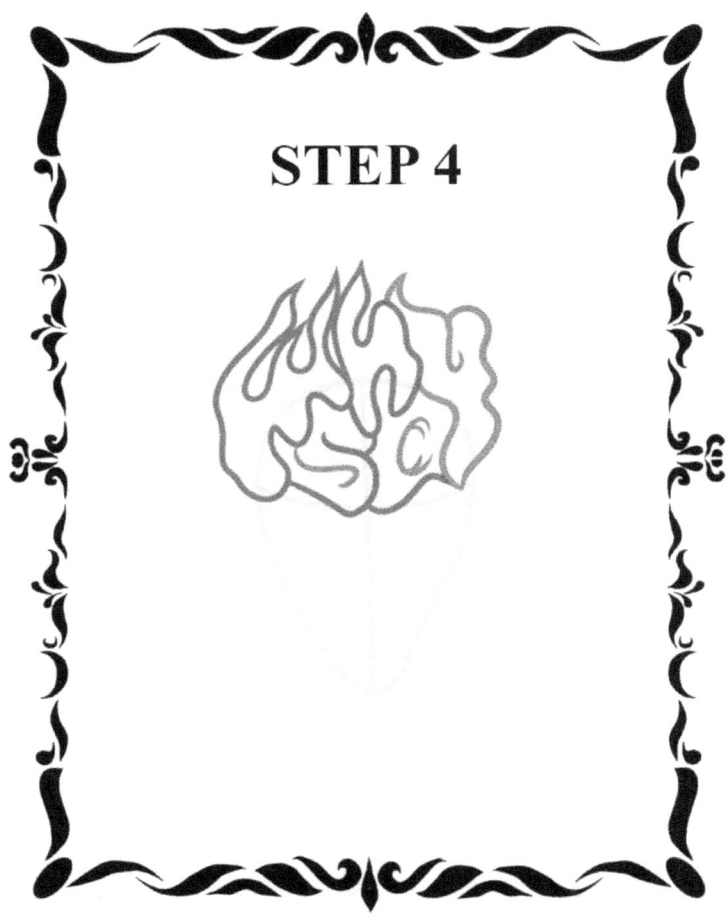

STEP 5

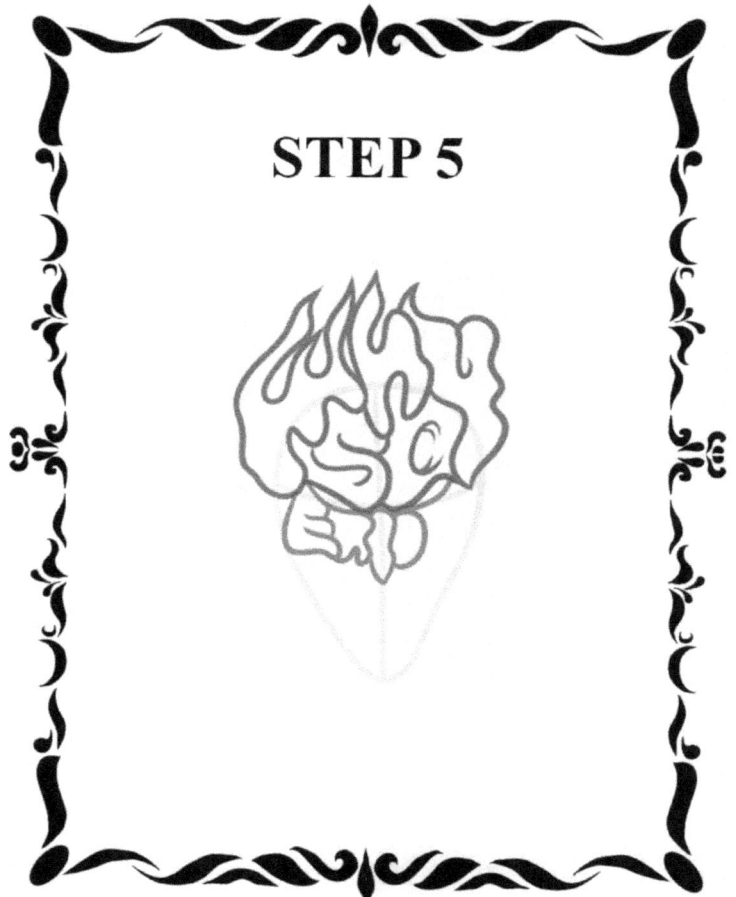

STEP 6

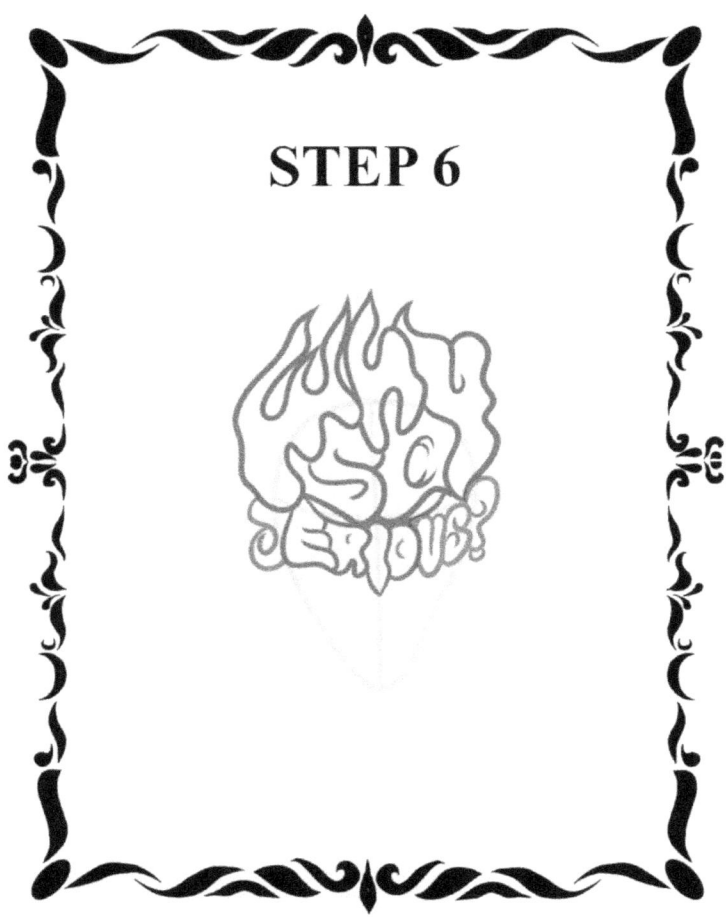

STEP 7

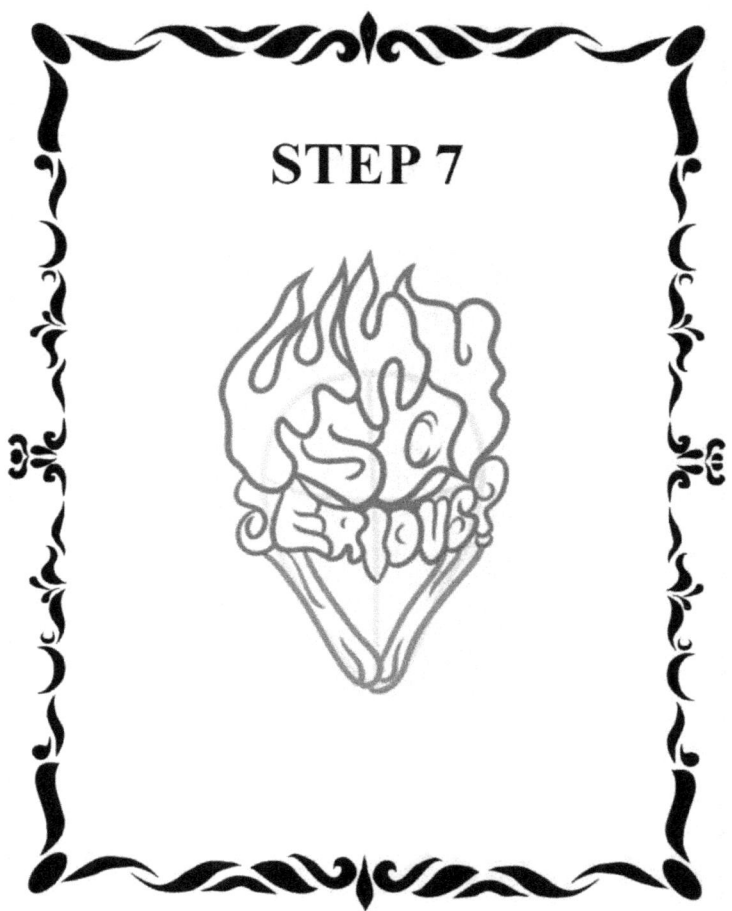

STEP 8

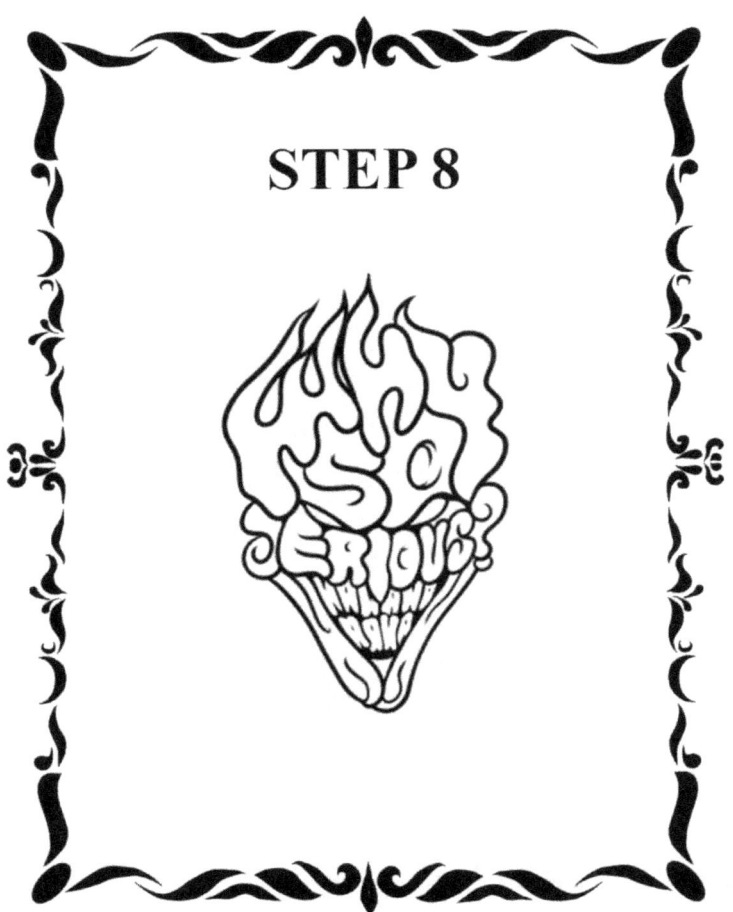

KOKOPELLI
TATTOO

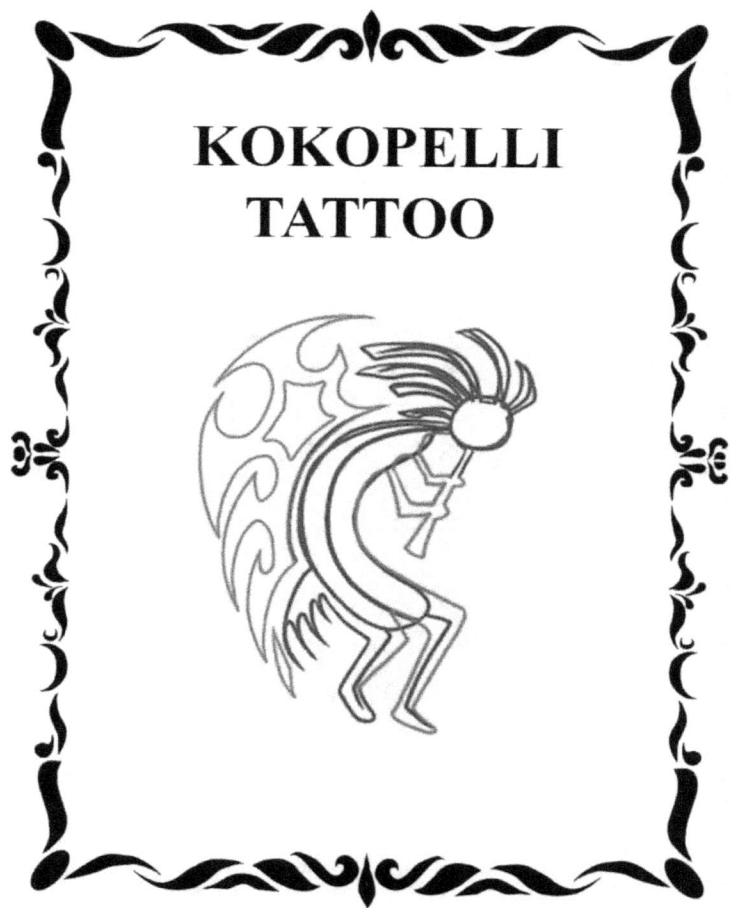

STEP 1

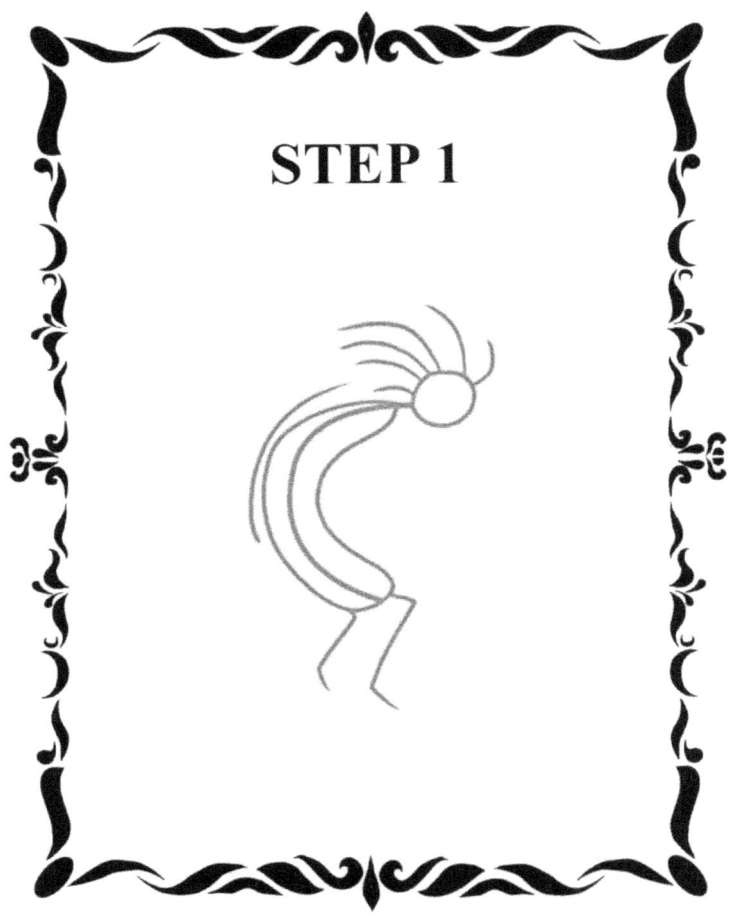

STEP 2

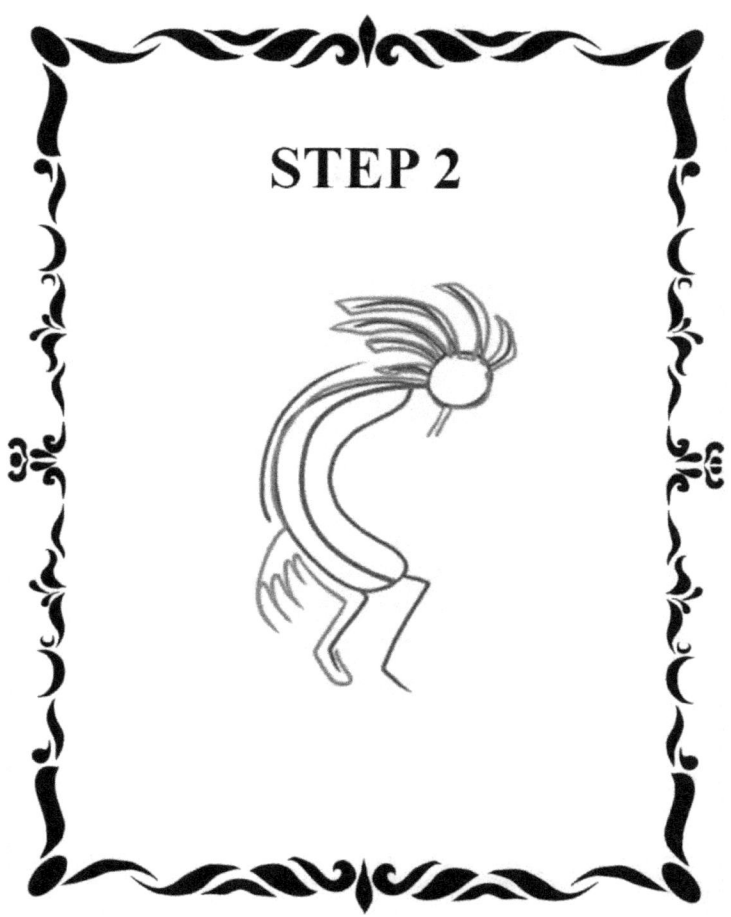

STEP 3

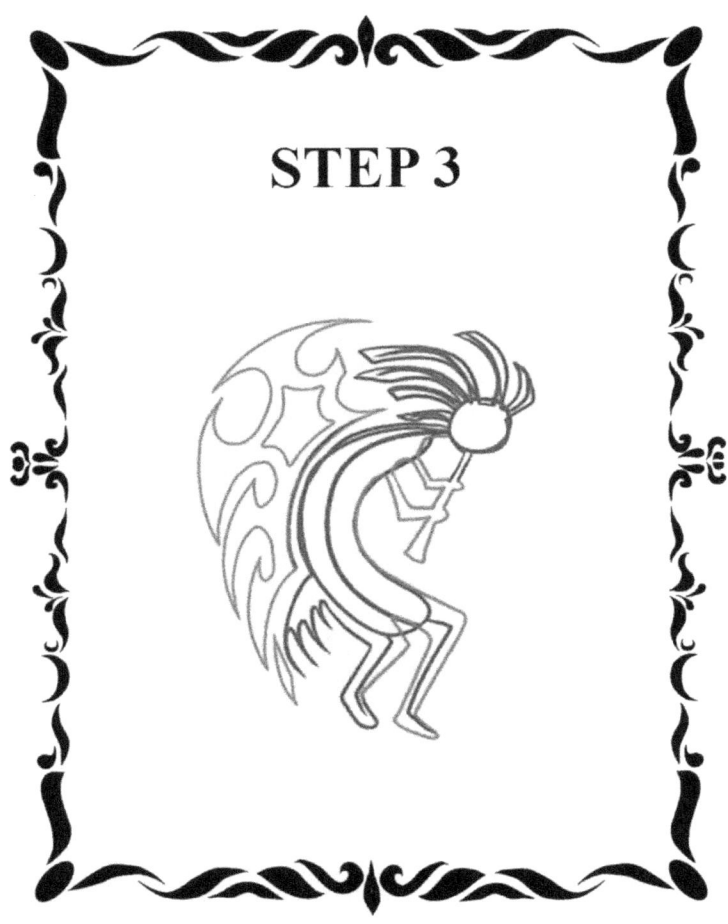

PETER PAN
TATTOO

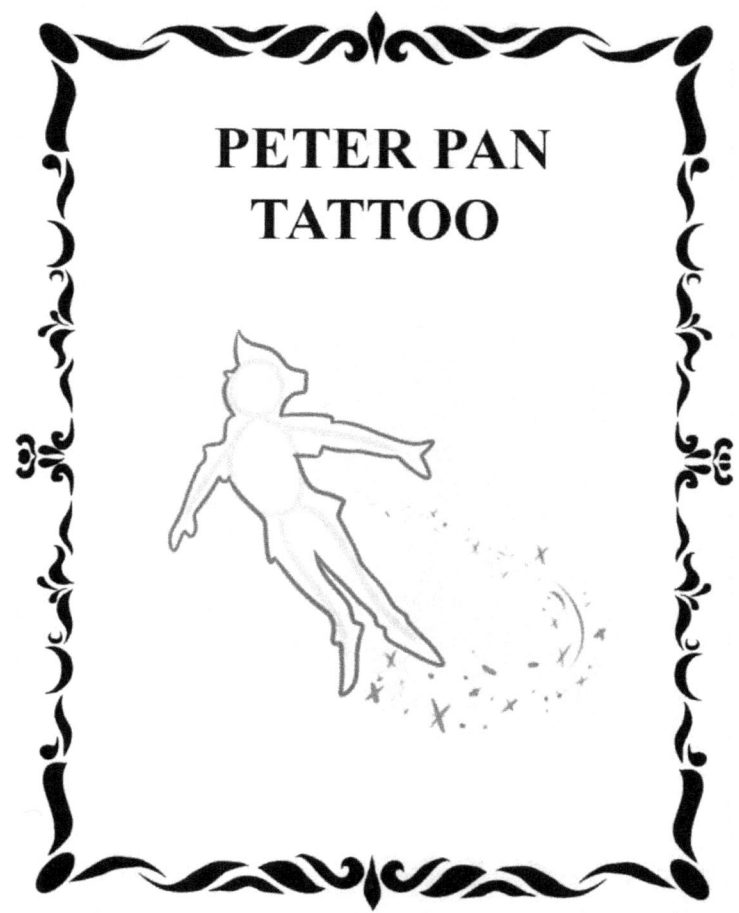

STEP 1

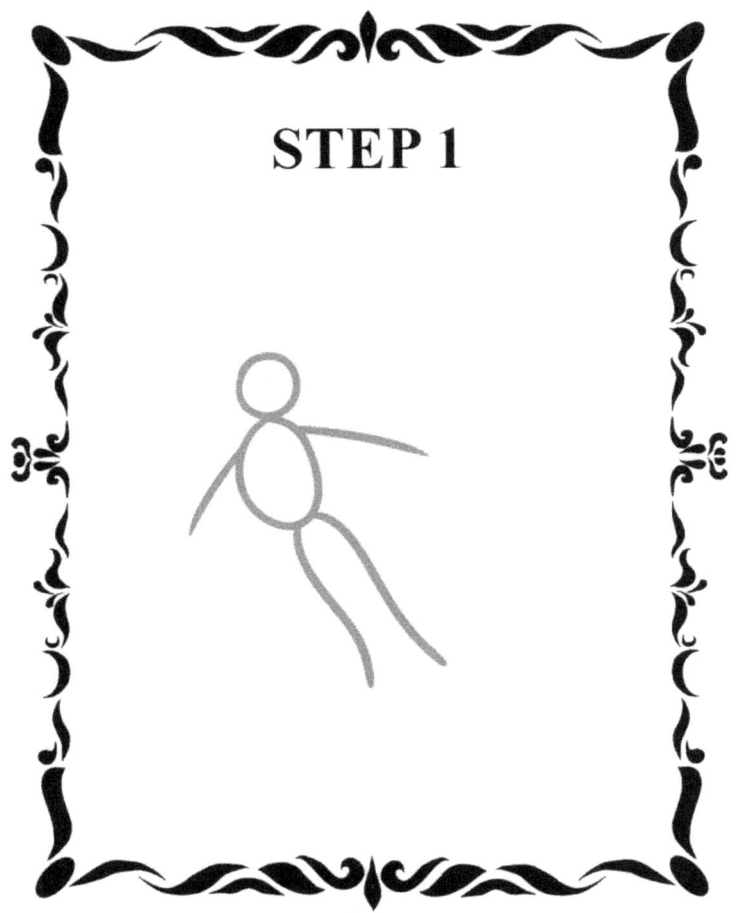

STEP 2

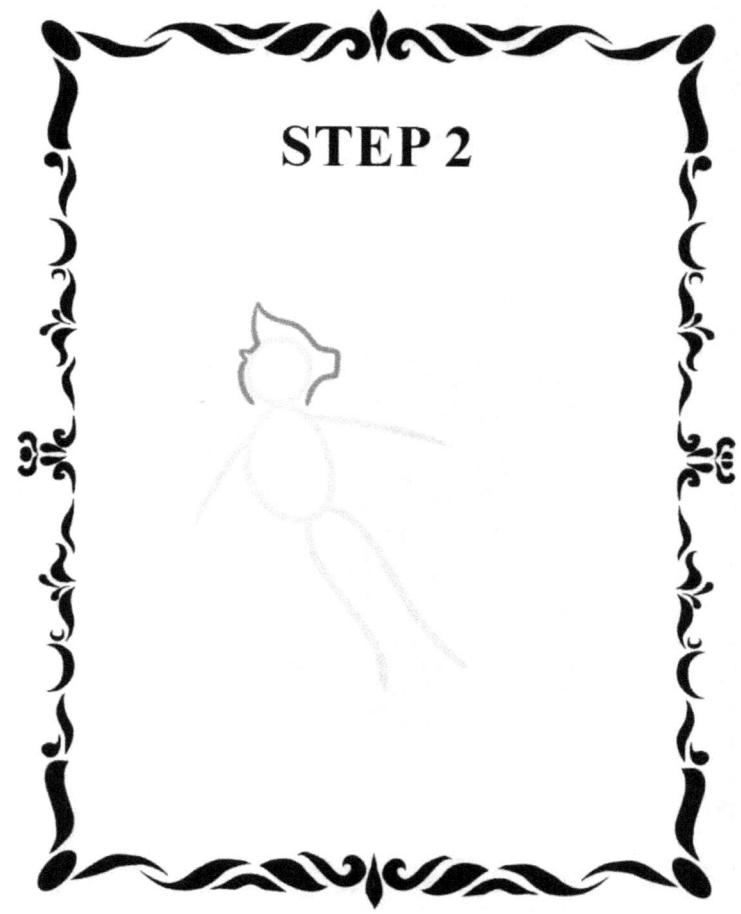

STEP 3

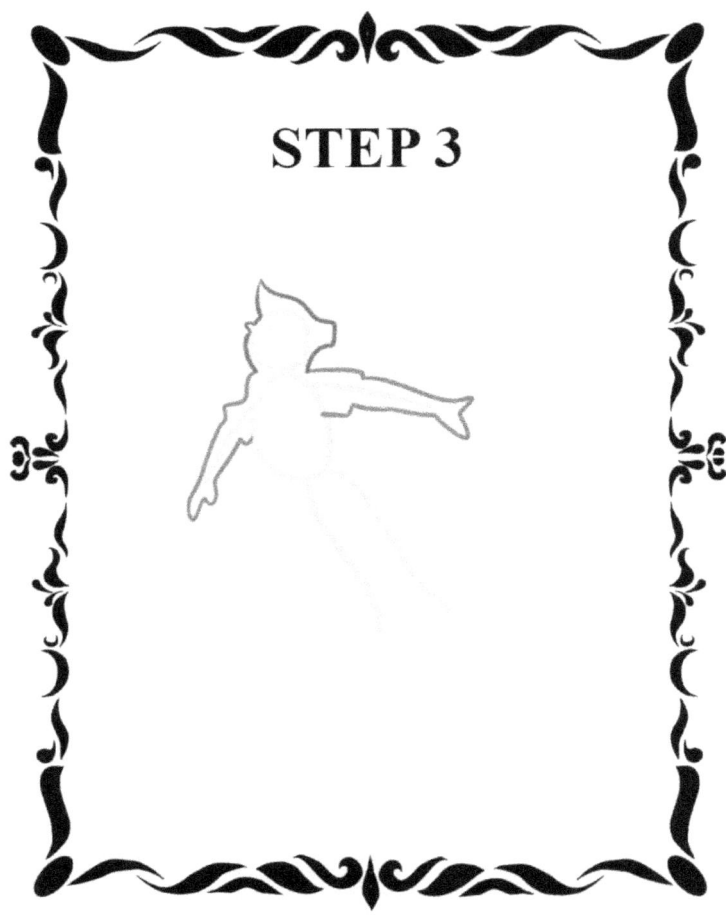

STEP 4

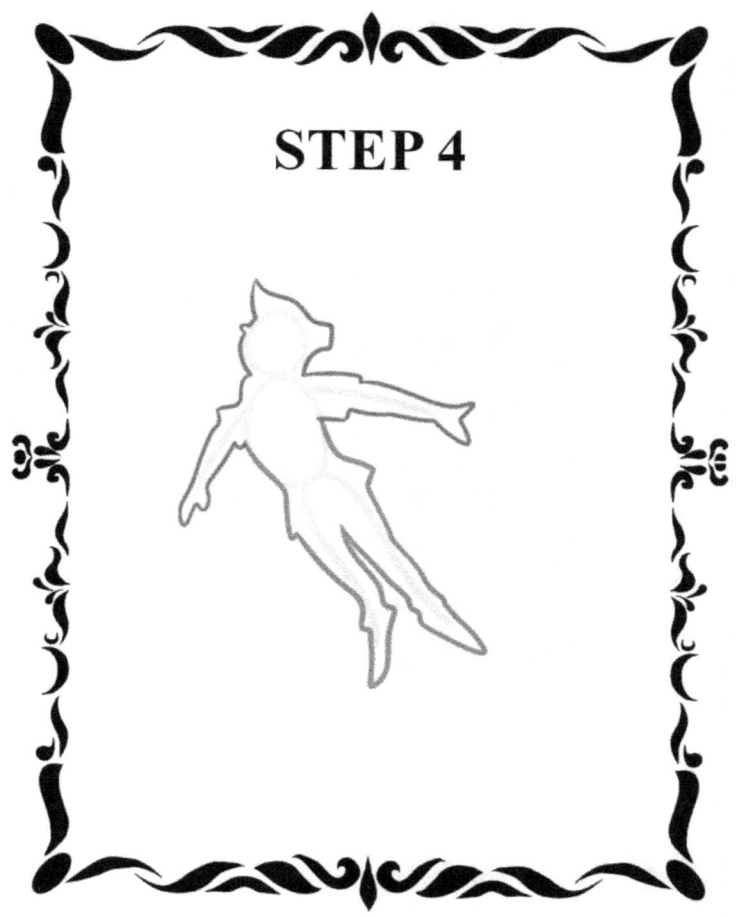

STEP 5

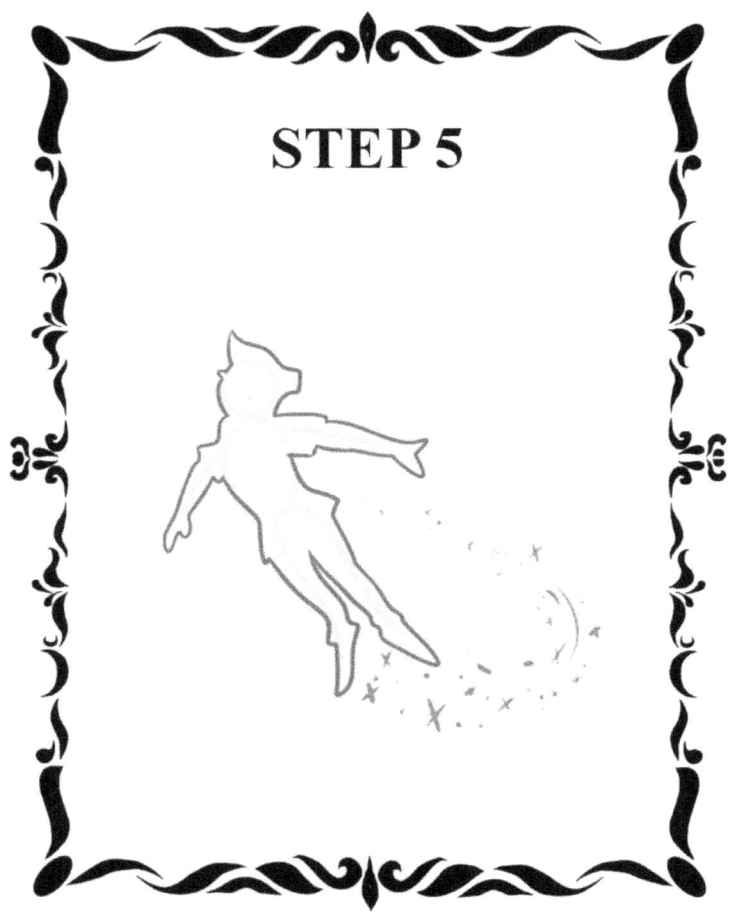

POSEIDON TATTOO

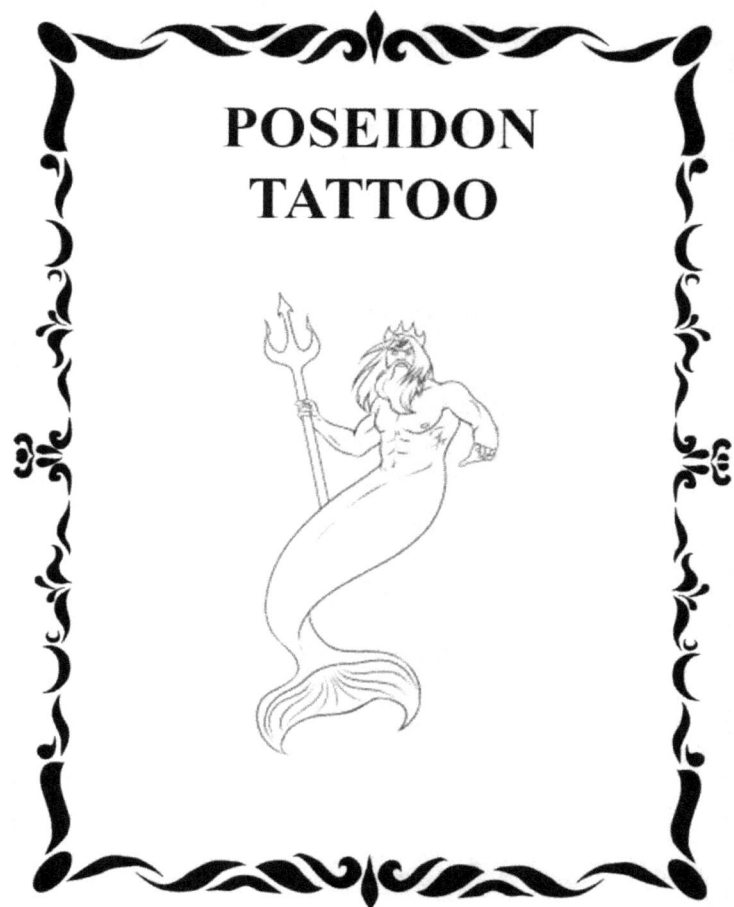

STEP 1

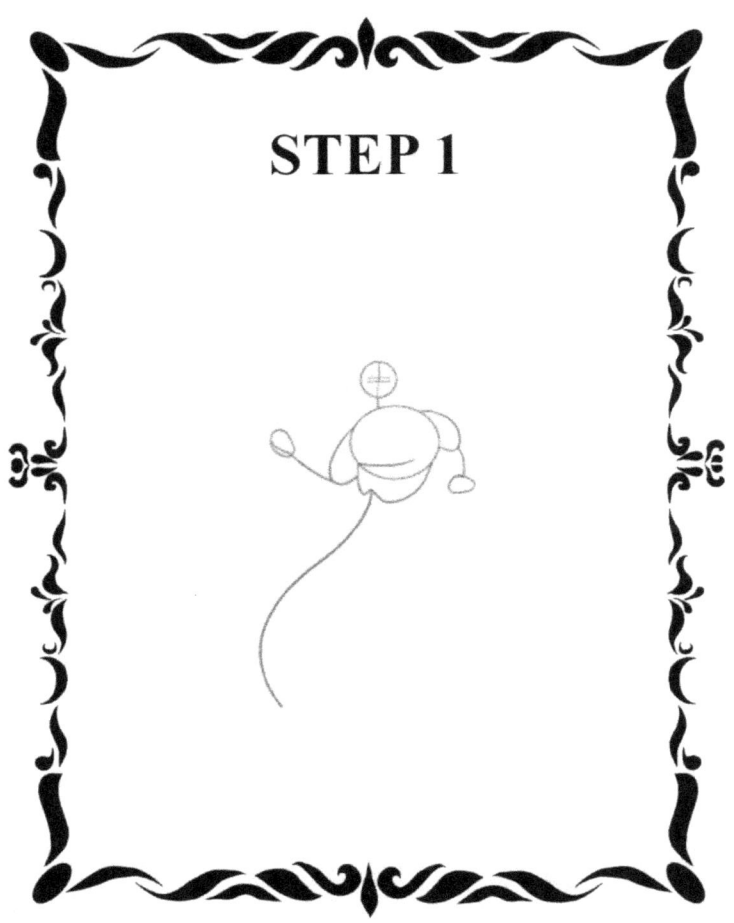

STEP 2

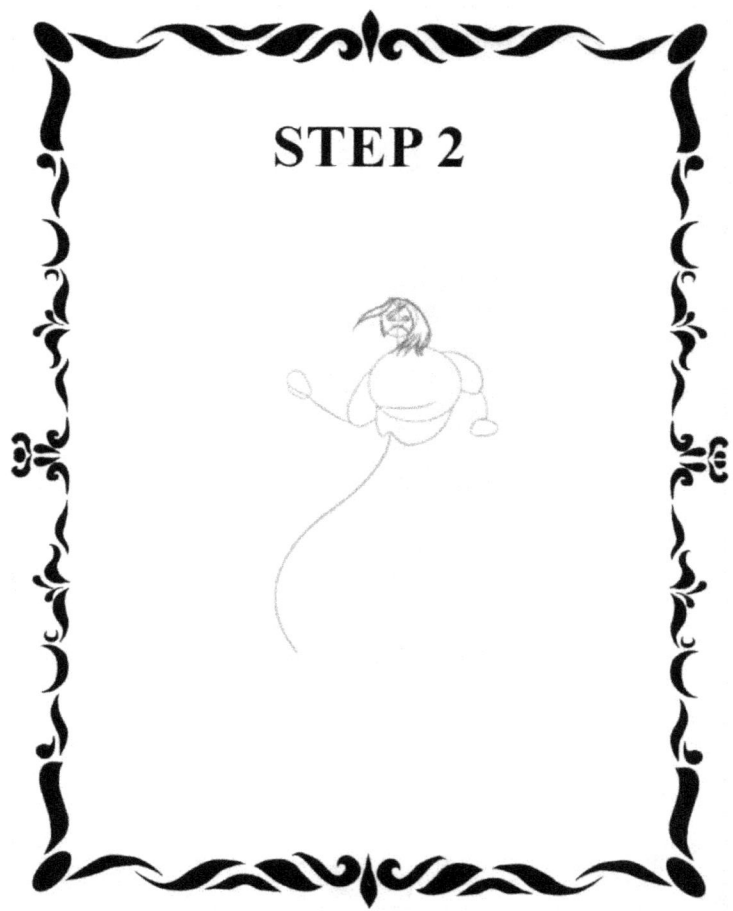

STEP 3

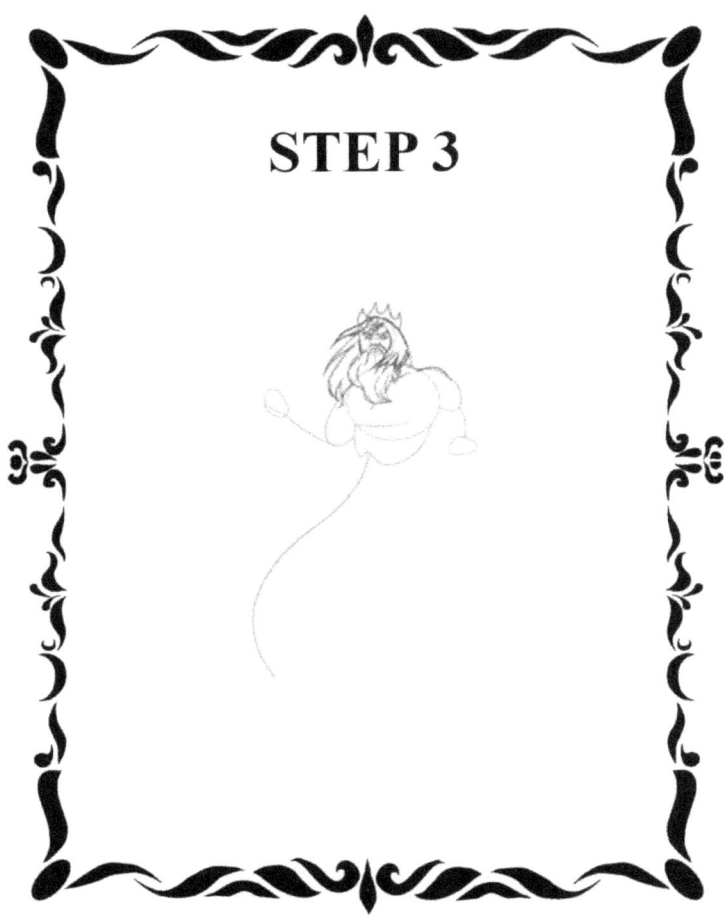

STEP 4

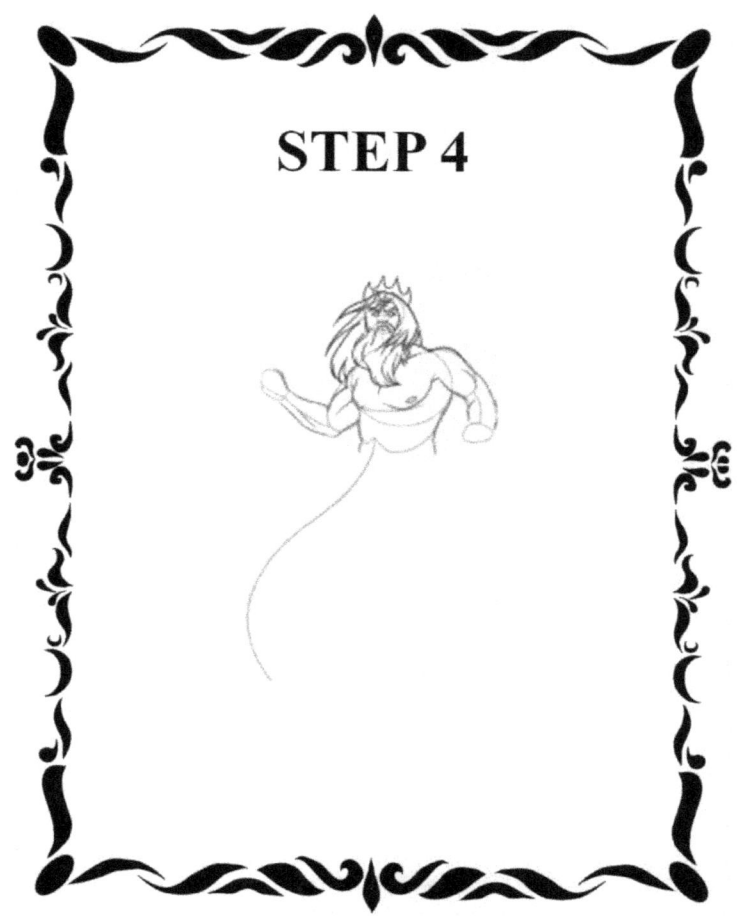

STEP 5

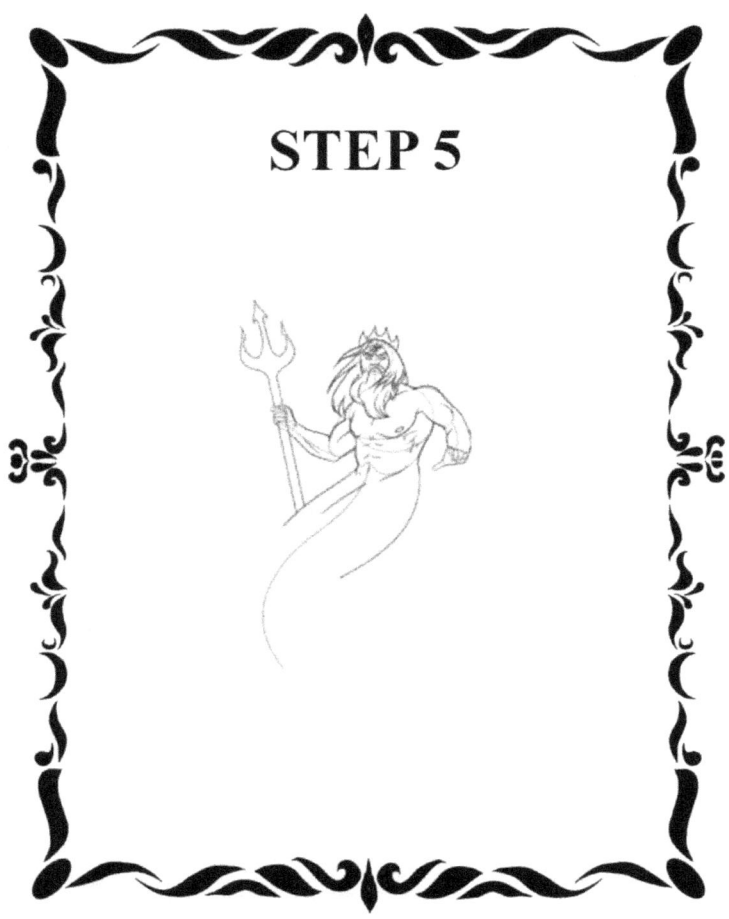

STEP 6

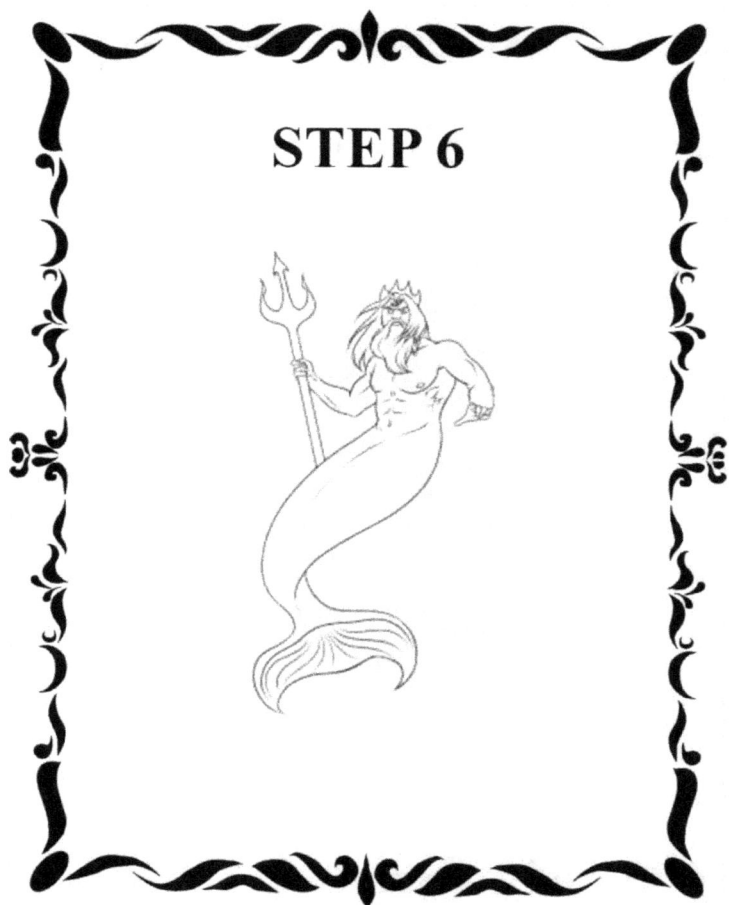

TAZ TATTOO

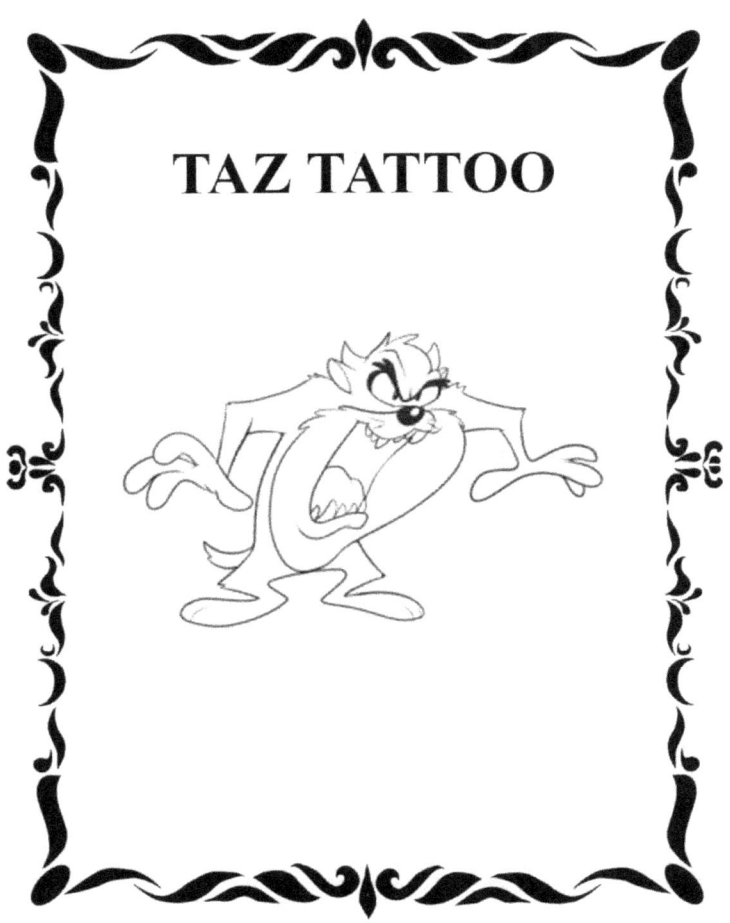

STEP 1

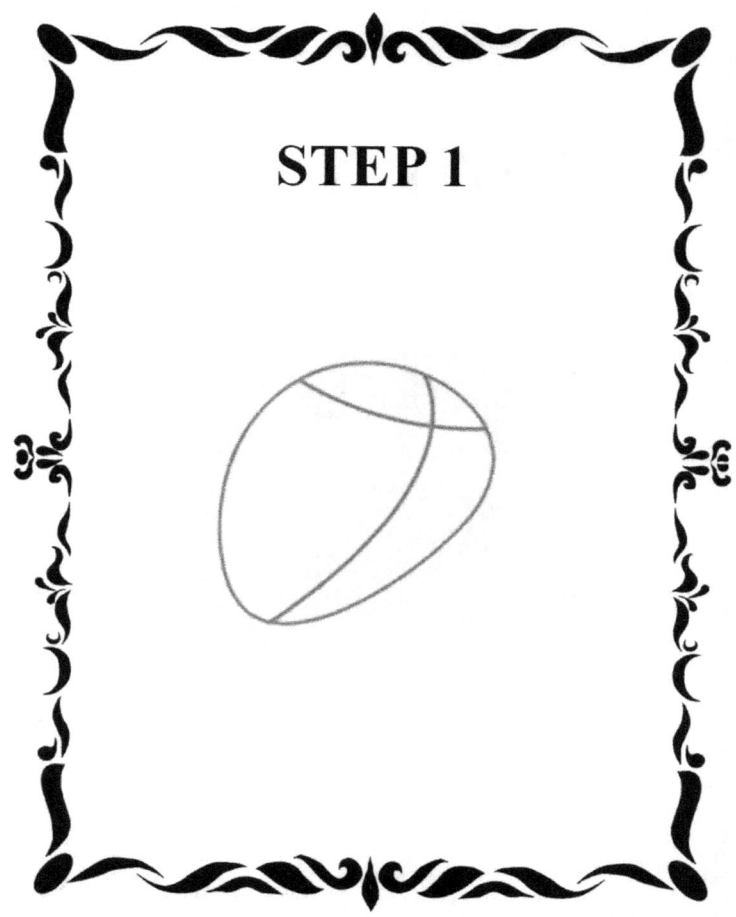

STEP 2

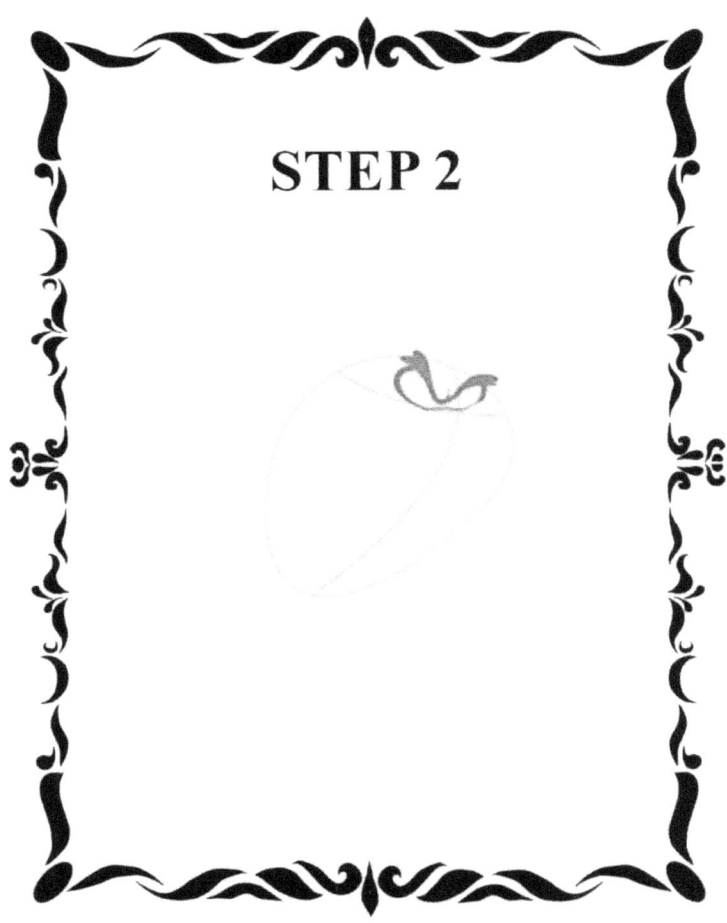

STEP 3

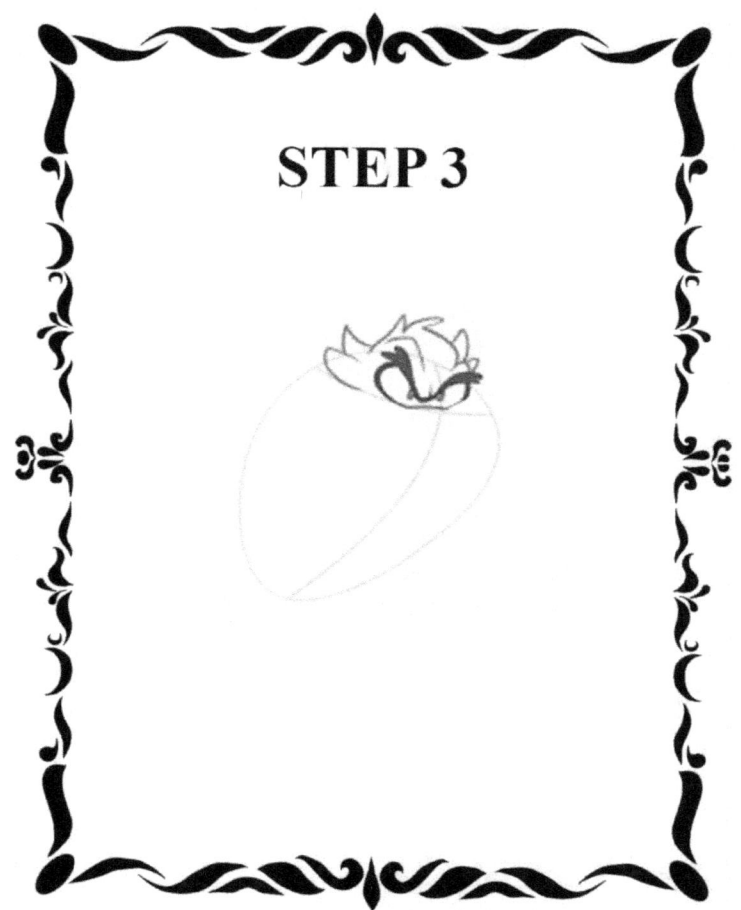

STEP 4

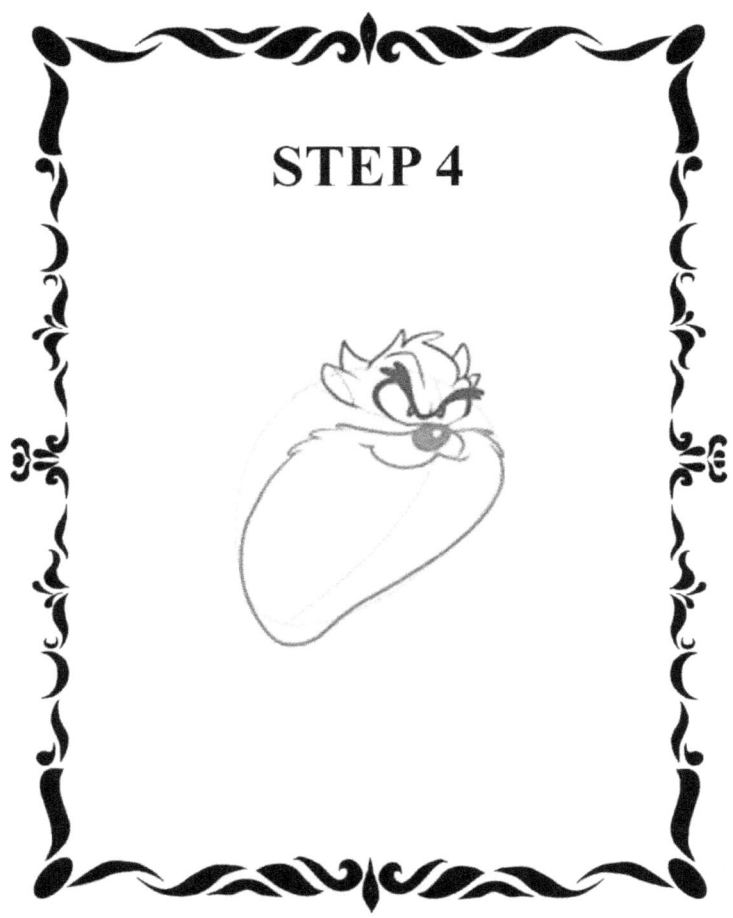

STEP 5

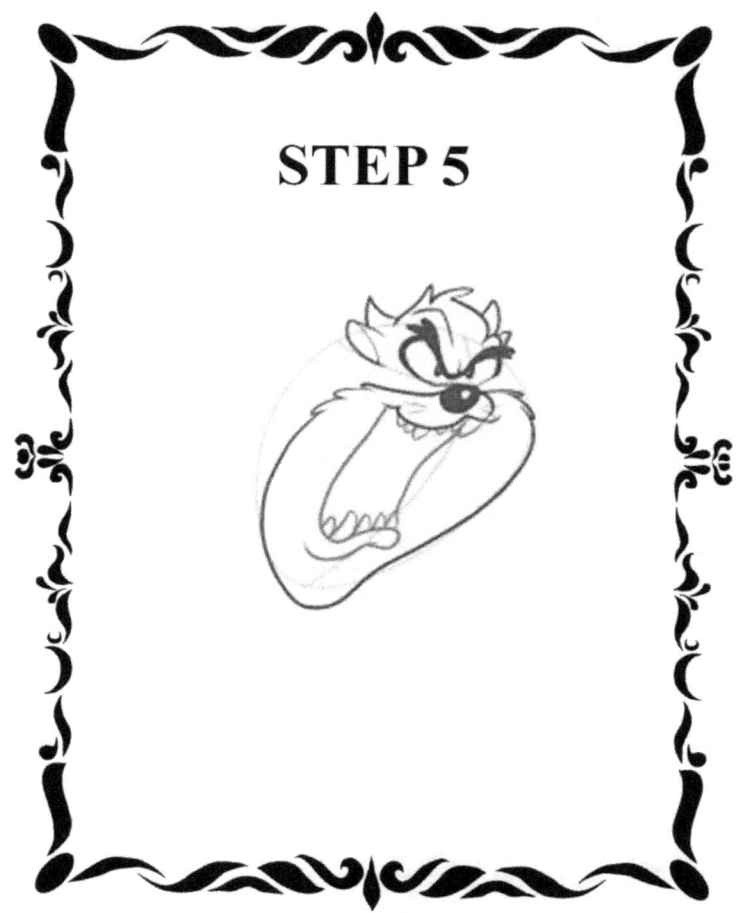

STEP 6

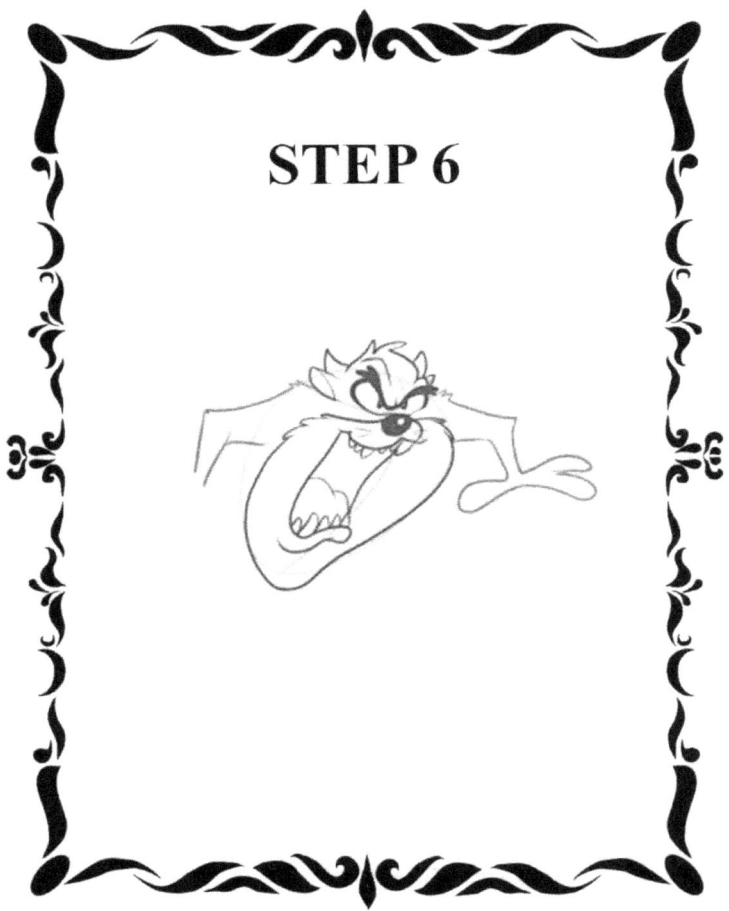

STEP 7

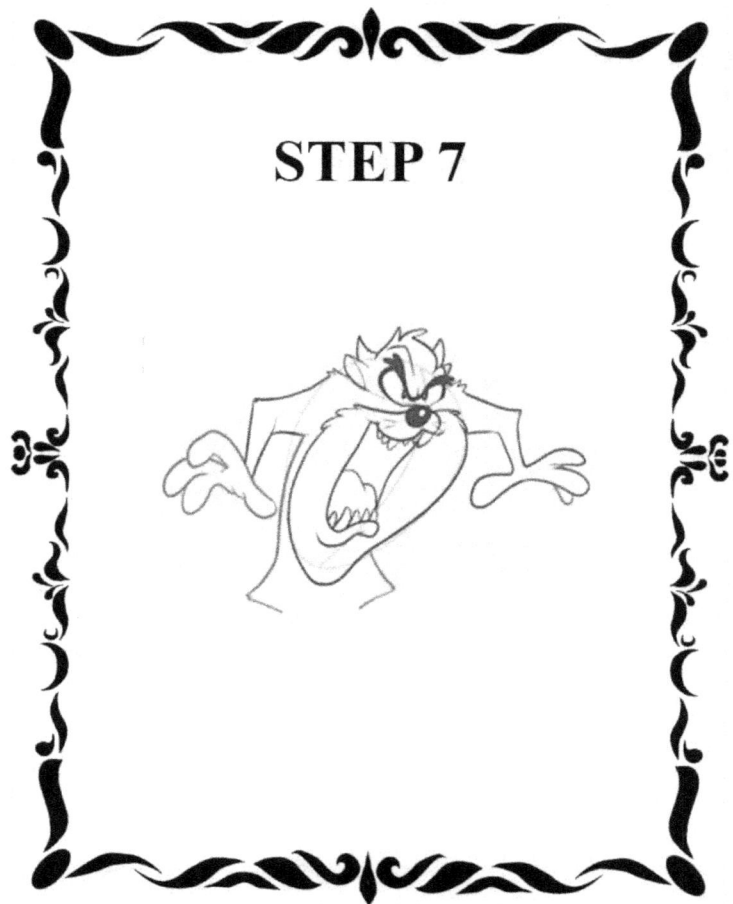

STEP 8

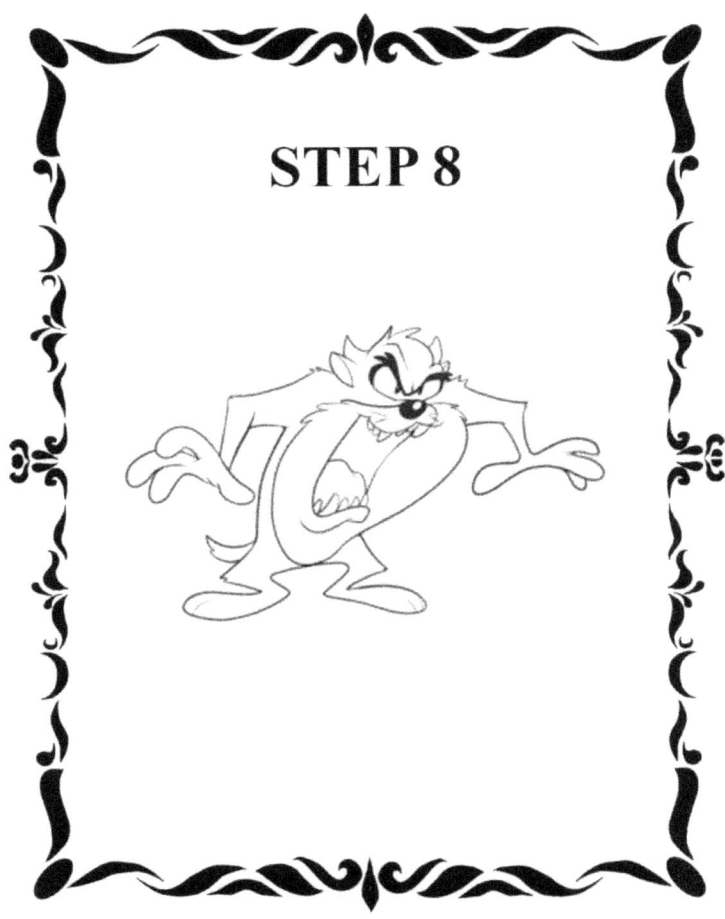

VALKRIE TATTOO

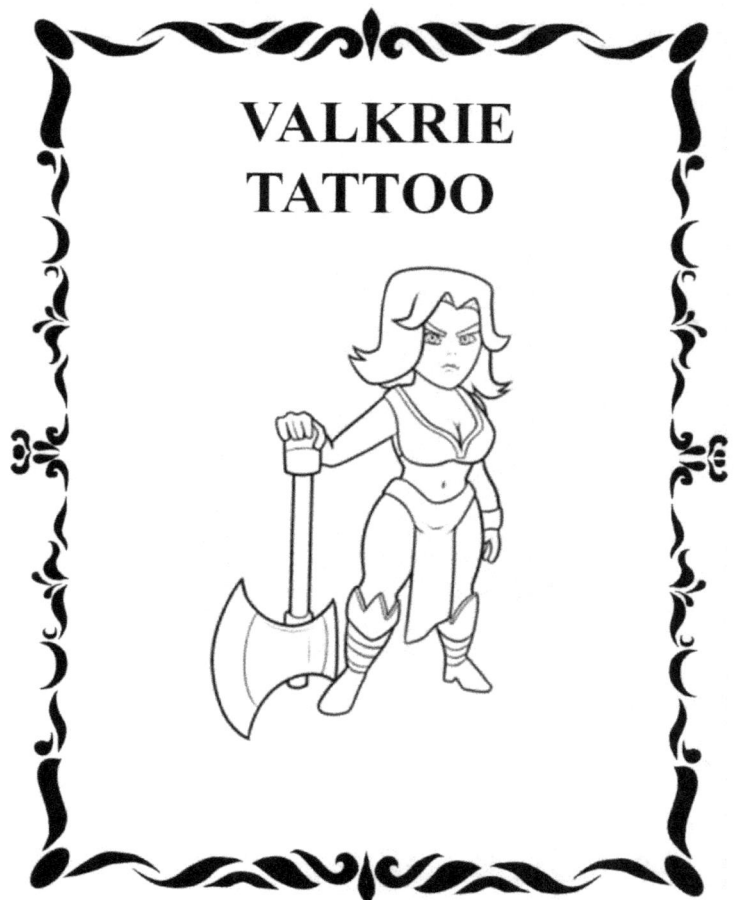

STEP 1

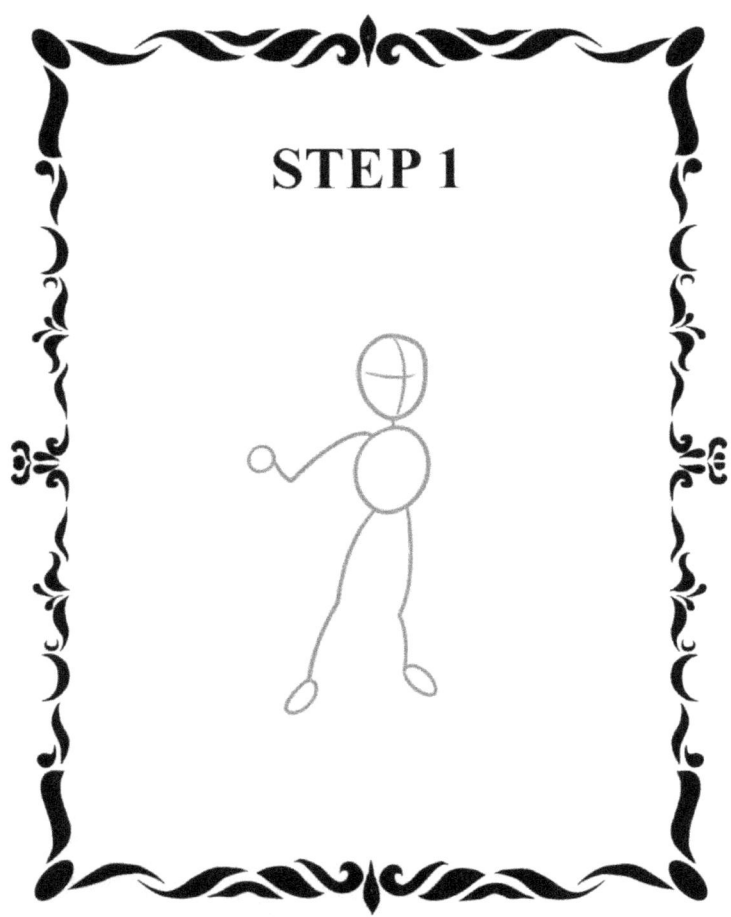

STEP 2

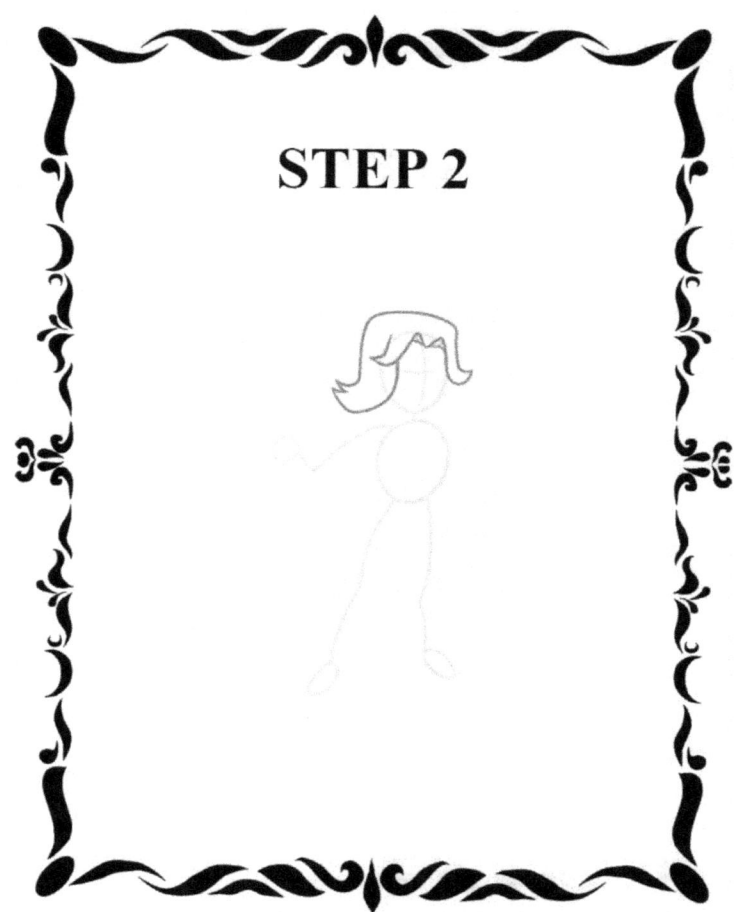

STEP 3

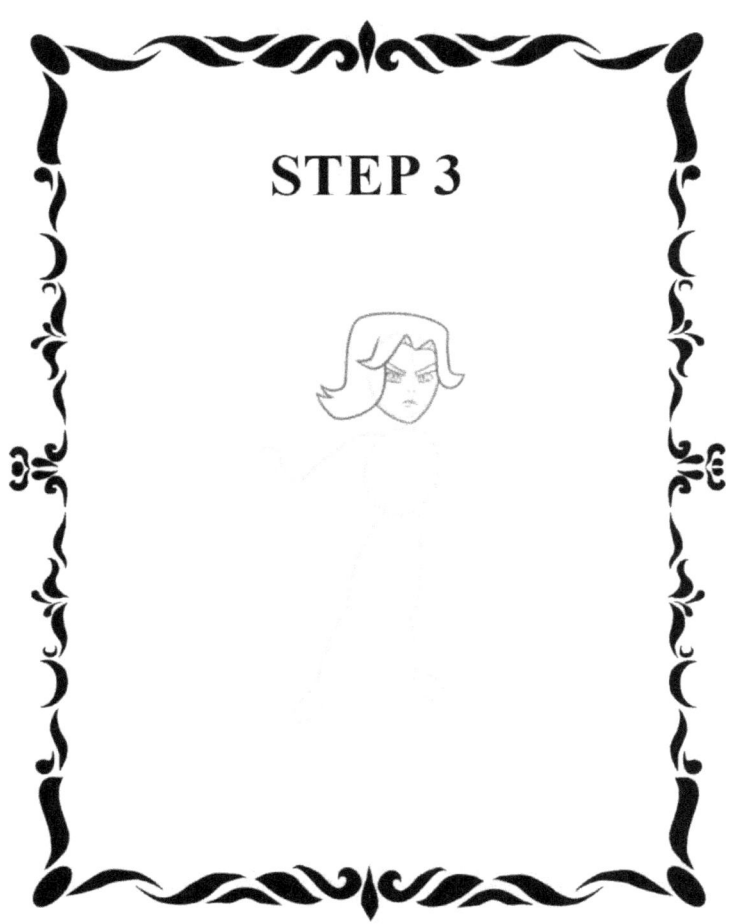

STEP 4

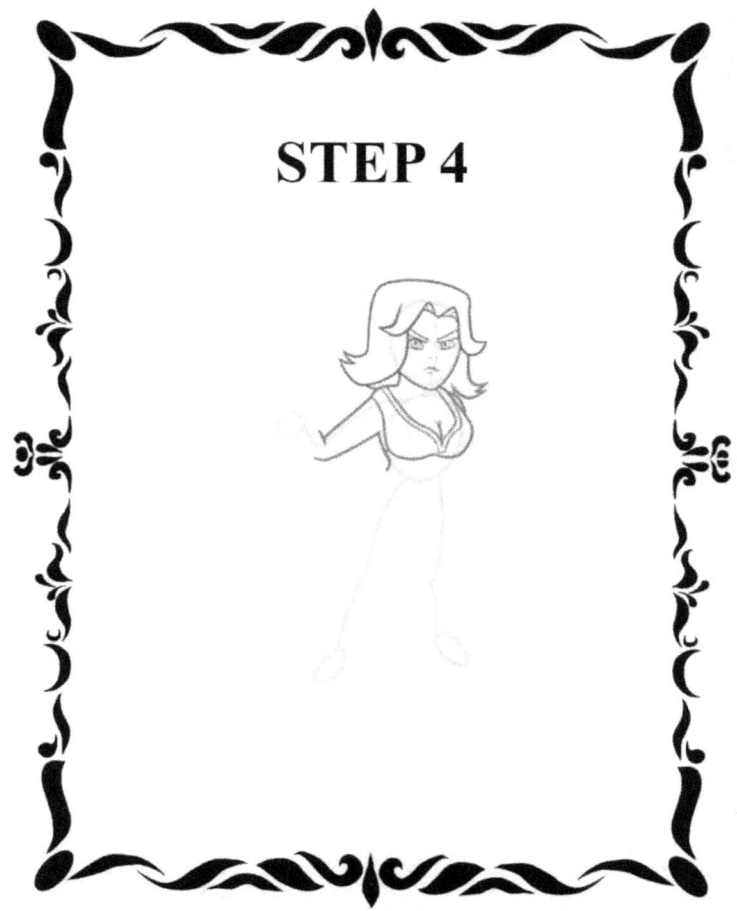

STEP 5

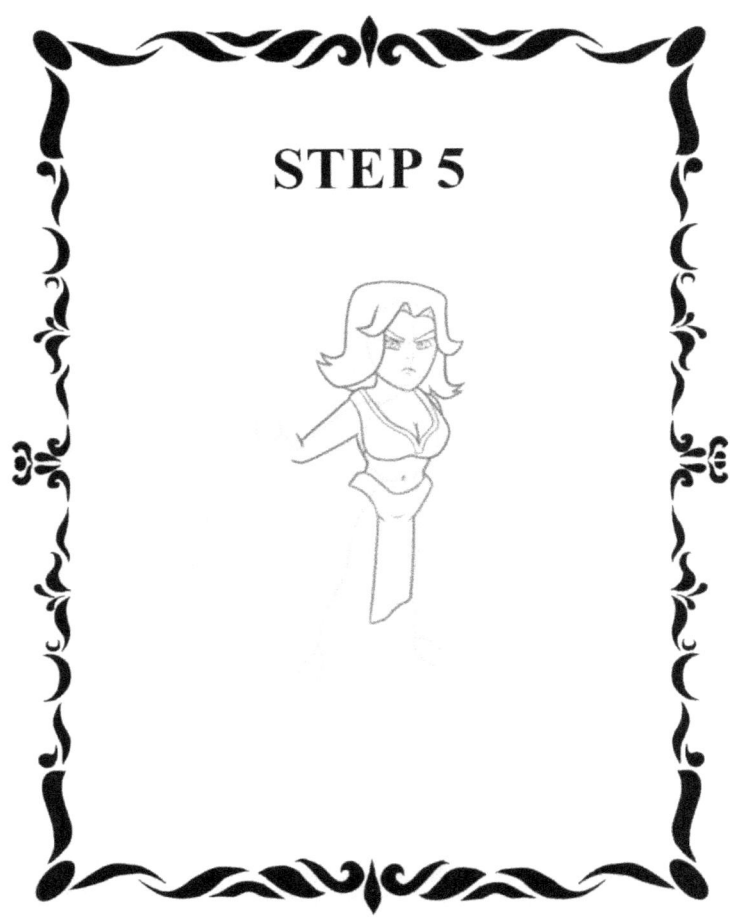

STEP 6

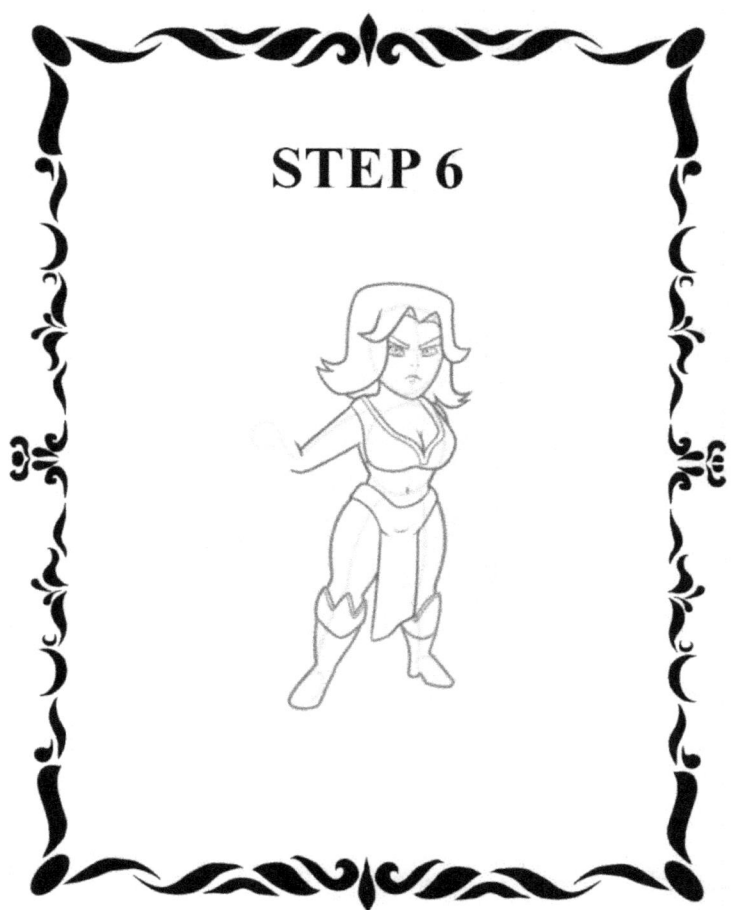

STEP 7

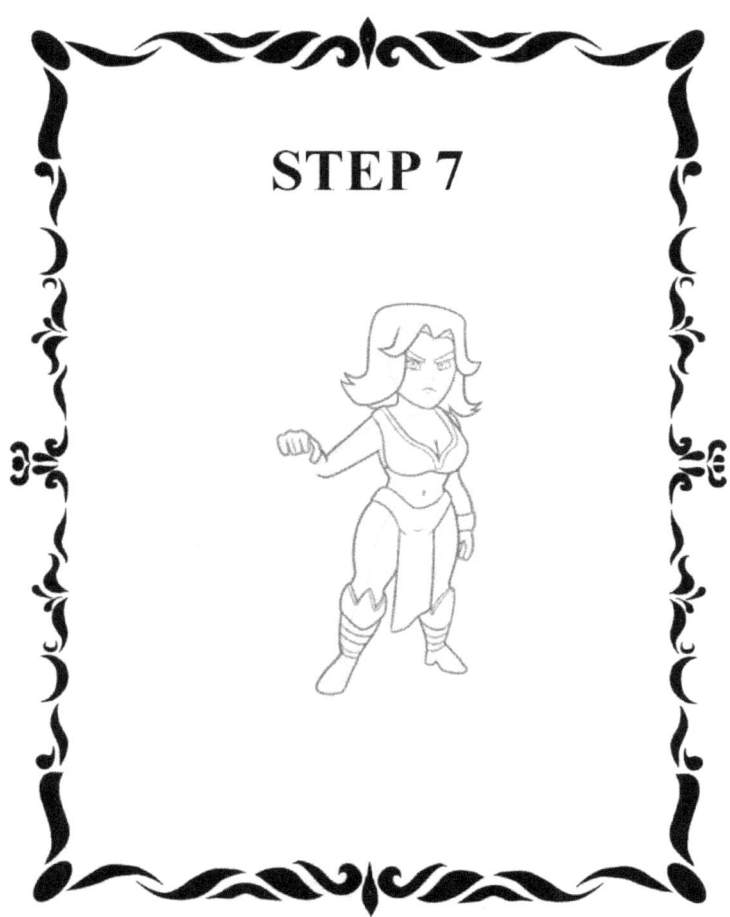

STEP 8

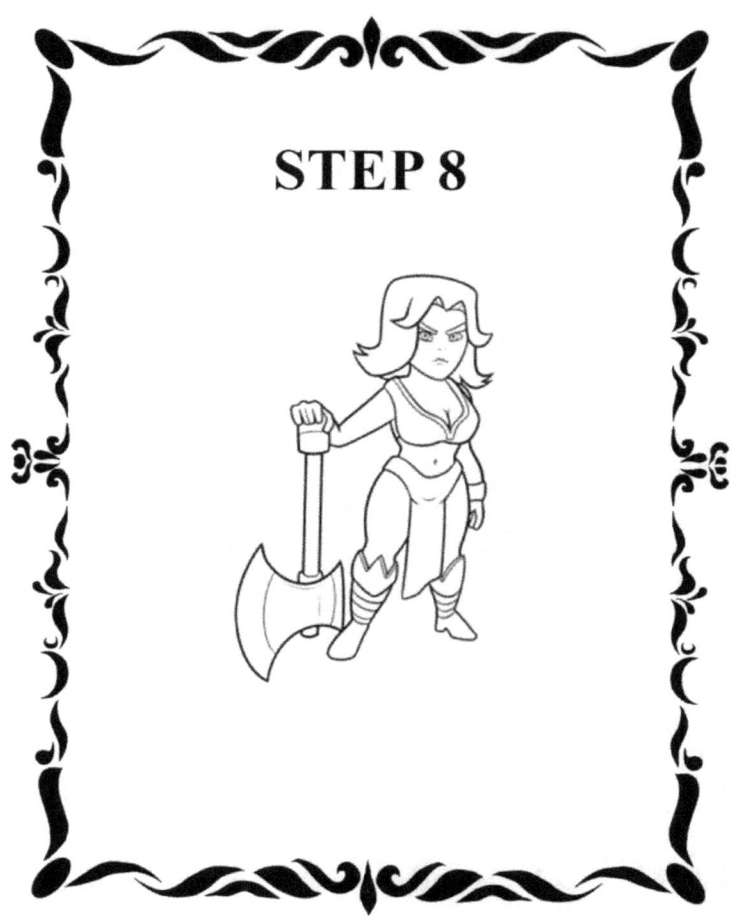

VIKING TATTOO

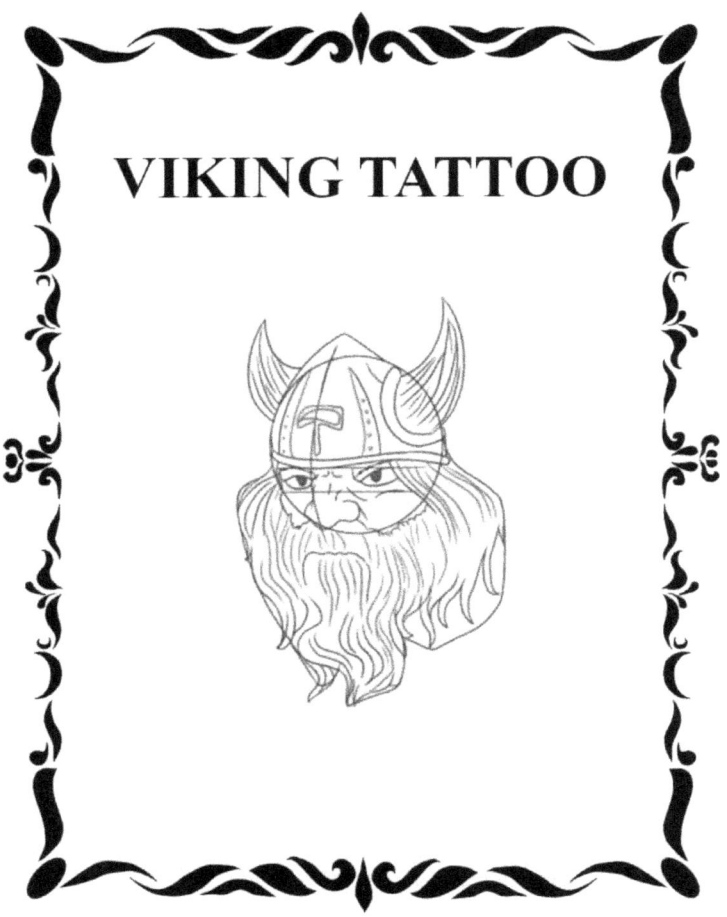

STEP 1

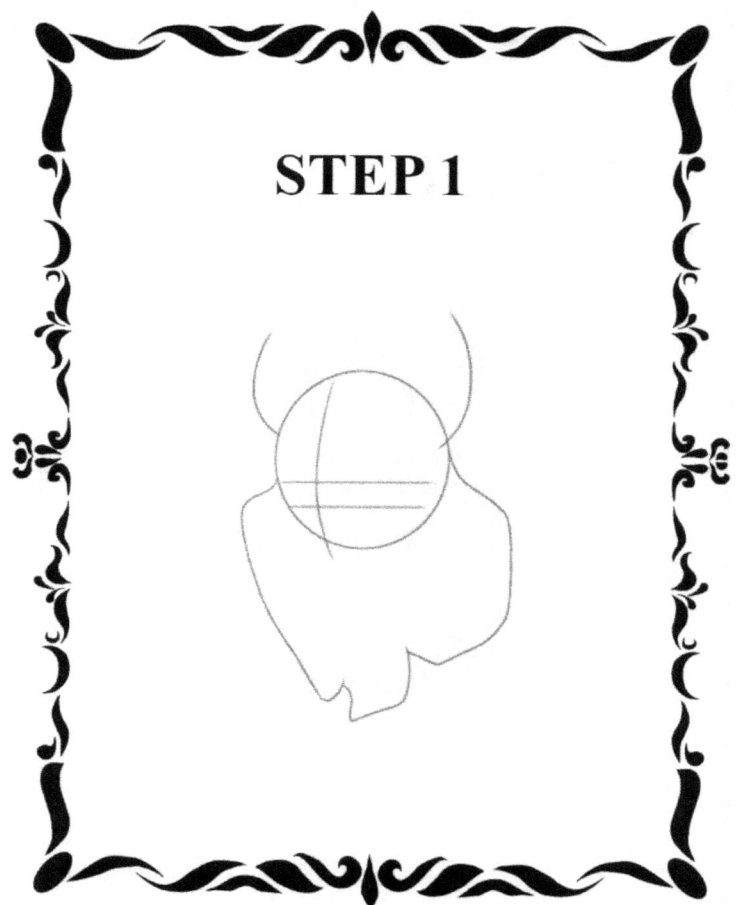

STEP 2

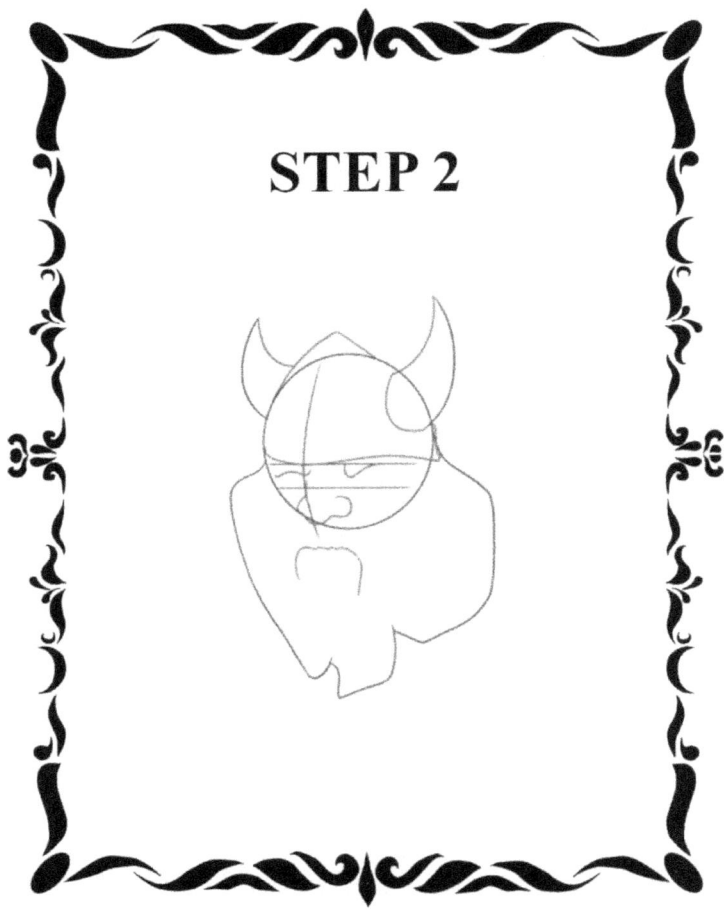

STEP 3

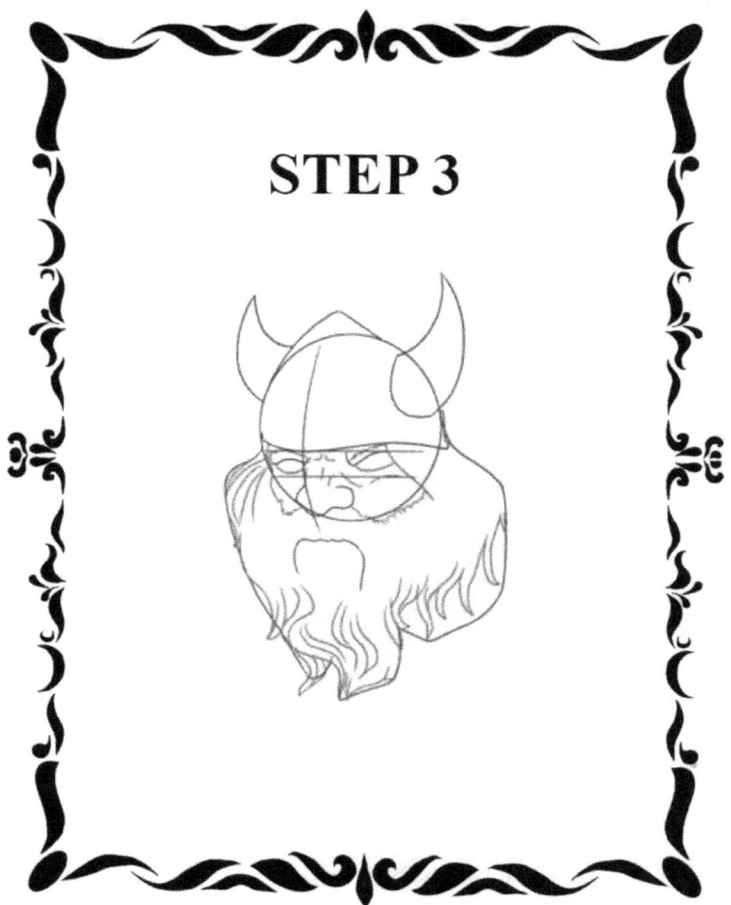

STEP 4

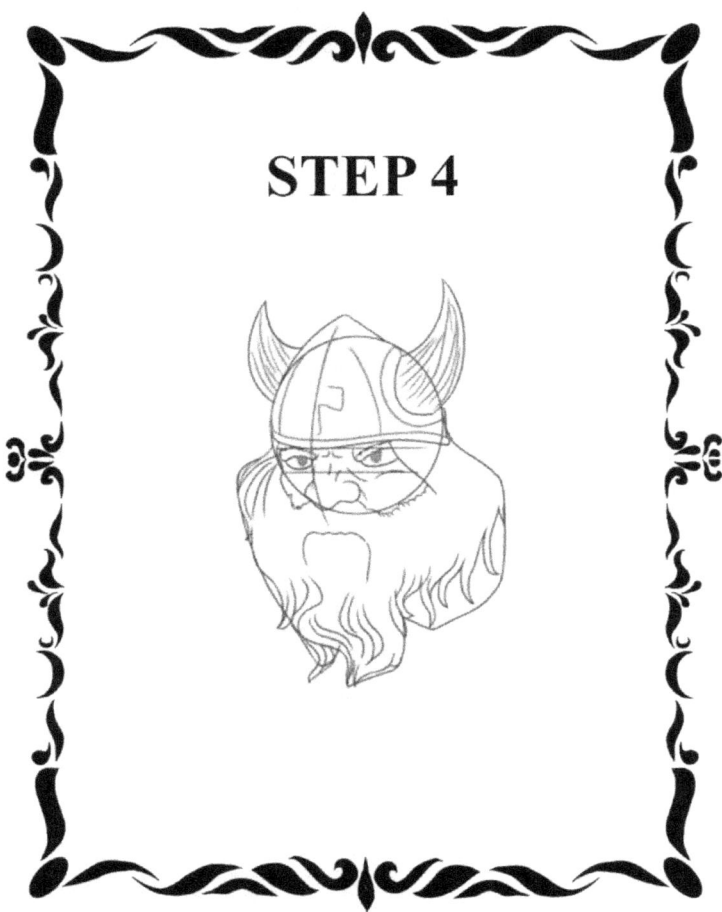

STEP 5

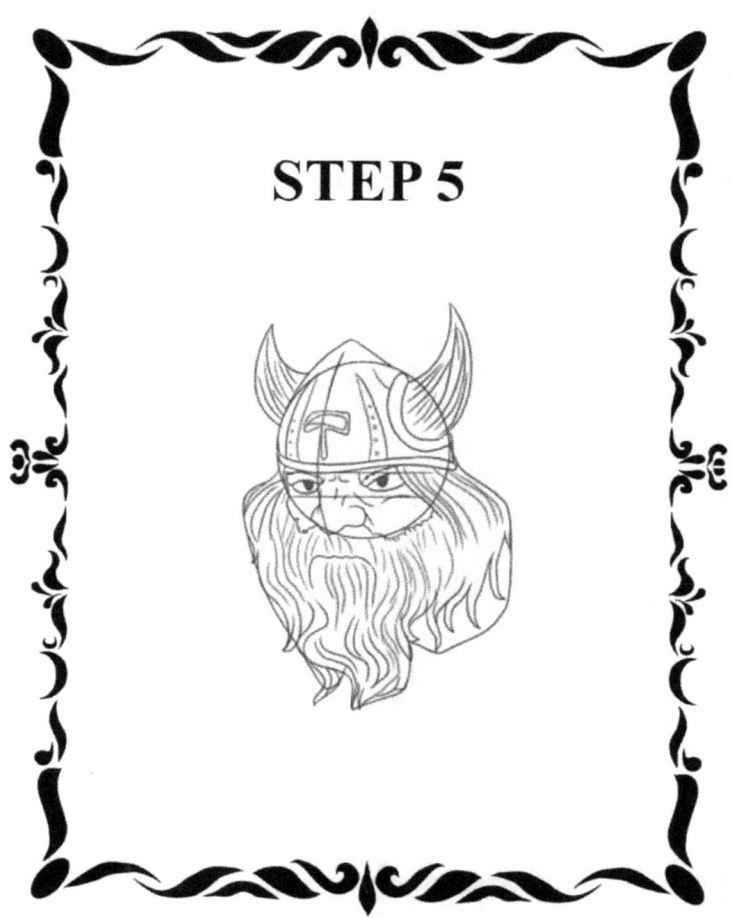